Soffritto

Soffritto

Tradition and Innovation in Tuscan Cooking

Benedetta Vitali

Photography by Cary Wolinsky

TEN SPEED PRESS
BERKELEY/TORONTO

A Kirsty Melville Book

1❿ Ten Speed Press
PO Box 7123
Berkeley, California 94707
www.tenspeed.com

Produced by Michael Melford

Distributed in Australia by Simon and Schuster Australia, in Canada by Ten Speed Press
Canada, in New Zealand by Southern Publishers Group, in South Africa by Real Books,
in Southeast Asia by Berkeley Books, and in the United Kingdom and Europe by Airlift
Book Company.

Cover and text design by Barbara Wolinsky, Trillium Studios, Norwell, Masssachusetts
Photography by Cary Wolinsky, www.carywolinsky.com

Some of the recipes in this book include raw eggs, meat, or fish. When these foods are
consumed raw, there is always the risk that bacteria, which is killed by proper cooking, may
be present. For this reason, when serving these foods raw, always buy certified salmonella-
free eggs and the freshest meat and fish available from a reliable grocer, storing them in the
refrigerator until they are served. Because of the health risks associated with the consump-
tion of bacteria that can be present in raw eggs, meat, and fish, these foods should not be
consumed by infants, small children, pregnant women, the elderly, or any people who may
be immunocompromised.

Library of Congress Cataloging-in-Publication Data

Vitali, Benedetta.
    Soffritto: tradition and innovation in Tuscan cooking / by Benedetta Vitali;
    photographs by Cary Wolinsky.   p. cm.
    Includes index.
    ISBN 1-58008-258-0
    1. Cookery, Italian—Tuscan style. I. Title.
TX723.2.T86 V57 2001
641.5945'5—dc21   2001003752

First printing, 2001
Printed in China

1 2 3 4 5 6 7 8 9 10 — 05 04 03 02 01

To My Children
Giuditta
Giacomo
Giulio
Duccio

contents

preface

I've lost count of how many times I've rewritten the introduction to this book. None of them seemed satisfactory; none explained, to me especially, why I had written it. Frustrating hours spent before the glowing screen, empty or with only a few abandoned lines, reinforced my growing conviction that the manuscript's best destiny was at the bottom of a drawer.

And when I roused myself from cathode-ray hypnosis, I reflected that there was really no need to add words to the infinite literature on cookery. Every slant on culinary knowledge had already been dealt with abundantly, and however I turned the frittata—excuse the tired metaphor—I found there was nothing new to report. My effort seemed entirely superfluous and irrelevant.

God, how boring! Who gives a damn about cooking?

One morning, I was trying with renewed spirit to make a bit of headway—and wearing out the floorboards of my study between the chair and window. I happened to glance out at the people doing their shopping in the Sant'Ambrogio market below my apartment, at the fruit and vegetable stalls that are now becoming endangered species. Suddenly, I was entranced.

I gazed down on those quickly moving figures of men and women, bright with color, laden with bags, bundles, and packages from which peeped celery leaves and artichoke stems. An old man had loaded onto the crossbar of his bicycle a great box of tomatoes, the red, mature ones used to make sauce for the winter, and by a miracle of balance he was managing to push the pedals with his legs bowed wide.

The mushroom stall was full of people and beautiful homegrown fungi, a luxury for Sunday's lunch. Grapes, figs, and the first pomegranates told me the cold weather was about to begin. In my mind I caught the aroma of roasted chestnuts that before long would envelop the streets of Florence, drifting out of the hot paper packets sold to shivering pedestrians.

And so, well, yes, perhaps it was beginning to rise to the surface, slowly, slowly: the deep sense of my connection with cooking.

♦

By midmorning, the Central Market of Florence bustles with shoppers searching for the best produce. Ripe tomatoes (left) and grapes (above) are just a few of the market's offerings.

I envisioned the man with the bicycle returning to his wife, both of them pensioners. She would have cleared enough space in the kitchen to prepare for the ritual of making the *pomarola*. The washed jars would be standing upside down in orderly rows; the great kettle used only for that occasion would be waiting ready on the stove.

"You got the basil, eh? These tomatoes look a little watery to me. Bah, we'll see, last year's were better. There, look up there, there's the apron."

"Maria, last year's are always better. Every year you say the same thing. You imagine they should be the ones we got twenty years ago, eh? You thought those were the nectar of the gods."

◆

"Oh, Grandmother! Mushrooms! Fry them for me."

"No, love, tomorrow we'll take them to the country and cook the caps on the embers of a campfire. Look how beautiful and firm they are. And with the stems I'll make us a risotto."

"Please, Grandma, I want them fried, they're better that way."

"All right, perhaps one, just for you. Look at this one. We'll put it aside and I'll fry it for you, but we won't tell anyone."

◆

Stories. These stories filled my mind—stories that carried with them atmospheres, smells, and memories. Tales ancient and recent, telling of lands and people; beautiful and ugly, joyous and sad stories that trace the woven fabric of my life.

With my nose pressed against the cold glass of my study window, I finally understood what attracted me to food. I could clearly see my intimate relationship with cooking, and with the many cuisines of the world. Cooking was my story, the one I knew best. It carried me forward and backward in my own life and connected me with all those other fascinating stories of distant, unknown lands.

To many, it may seem a sign of dubious mental health to first write a book and then ask why one has written it. Surely it would make more sense to do it the other way around. I believe my initial motivations were rather superficial. They were motivations that move many people I know to write: a search for gratification, economic expectations, and so forth. But as I wrote and the book began to exist and to contain a part of me, I could not help asking myself more seriously why it should end up on bookstore shelves.

The Sant'Ambrogio market attracts shoppers from all over Florence with the quality of its local produce and its friendliness.

Often I recalled the words of a person I love very much, a great eater and a master of life, who is fond of saying, "In Italy there are only two people left who have never written a book." These words made my initial motivations fade, and a sense of the ridiculous captured me and stole away all my enthusiasm. But I knew that this was something more than a simple list of recipes. I wanted to convey the feeling and the passion that I put into the act of cooking and this same passion that I sense when I watch others prepare a meal. I had to give this passion the dignity, weight, and value it deserves, and for a long time I could not.

I spun like a top among misleading and limiting definitions of Tuscan cuisine, the cuisine of the family, and the cuisine of memory, and notions of mental and nutritional balance. Every point of view left me with a sense of incompleteness; each was fragile because it was not mine.

But when I ask myself where those artichoke stems from the market would have gone, and who would have cooked them, and how; who would have eaten them; what the cook's house would be like, and the people who lived there: then I begin to imagine. I see a family chatting at the table in the evening:

"Mmm! Fried artichokes."

I see a nervous woman, with a thousand reasons for dissatisfaction, banging them down in the middle of the table. Prepared out of obligation, they are overcooked and have turned gray. Then I see a man who cooks them with care, waiting for someone to arrive to whom he can show such ability and dedication. And when I have seen a thousand possible stories in my mind's eye, finally I understand.

Maria's *pomarola*, Grandmother's mushrooms, the artichokes of who knows who—all have helped me understand: Food is a story, and like every good story it is worth the trouble of telling. It can be told and retold, like fairy tales to children. It helps us to wander between memories and fantasy. It reveals to us our private lives.

And so I told myself that mine was just one more story; but that was fine, because stories are always being told and will always be told.

A vendor pushes a heavy cart laden with fresh fruit and vegetables.

Soffritto

soffritto

THE BASICS OF TUSCAN COOKING

When I was eighteen, I discovered freedom, work, friendship, love, and … soffritto. I left home, bought a motor scooter, and got a part-time job at lunchtime. I felt free and able to do with myself whatever I pleased. I was happy, independent, and totally unencumbered with cooking skills, which I then believed to be of little consequence. I often think of that period of my life as one of the best. It was a time when I was adopted, as it were, by the family of the boy I had chosen. His was a family where people used to eat a lot, and well. I put on six pounds just in the first month. Mealtime was a true pleasure: we joked, we talked, and, you may believe it, we ate.

There I learned how to cook, and I believe that what caught my interest was how the woman who did the cooking in that family—later to become my mother-in-law—moved pots and pans about with levity, care, and relaxation, all at once. One could not help but see that she was looking forward to the pleasure of eating what she was making. She taught me how to make soffritto. She used to tell me that, once having learned it, I would be able to make practically everything, including soups, sauces, and stews. In Tuscany, soffritto is the starting point.

Several years have elapsed since the motor scooter, the freedom, and my first attempts in the kitchen. I feel obliged to pass this knowledge on to you, as my mother-in-law passed it to me, as her mother-in-law had passed it to her—as it has been passed down through the generations.

In Italian, soffritto means "under fried." A preparation of lightly-browned minced vegetables, soffritto is not a dish by itself. It is the foundation on which many Tuscan sauces, soups, and other dishes are built. At one time it was called "false ragout," because soffritto

◆

Benedetta at nineteen (left)

◆

A vendor in Sant'Ambrogio market selects porcini mushrooms for flavor, not for beauty. (above)

was thought to vaguely recall the flavor of meat sauce. Many of the sauces and other recipes that follow begin with a soffritto, made in a slightly different way in each case, depending on the dish. Here is a basic one:

AN ALL-PURPOSE

Soffritto

1 red onion
1 carrot, peeled
1 stalk celery
⅓ cup (75 ml) extra virgin olive oil

♦

Three soffrittos, each browned as needed, depending on the dish.

Mince the onion, carrot, and celery as finely as you can, using a knife or a *mezzaluna* (a crescent-shaped, double-handled knife). A food processor should not be used because it squashes the onion rather than chopping it, and the soffritto becomes a mush. Chopping an onion by hand might induce a few tears, but one should weep from time to time.

Choose a heavy-bottomed aluminum or tin-plated copper pan in order to brown the soffritto evenly, and heat the oil in the pan over a medium flame. You should use extra virgin olive oil: It works well at high temperatures and it is the most digestible of cooking oils. The amount you use will vary according to the quantity of vegetables; don't overdo it, but put in enough oil to ensure an even browning. Add the minced vegetables and sauté, stirring frequently, until the vegetables are the desired hue, which will vary depending on the recipe.

Never leave the soffritto unattended on the stove. It must be watched at all times and stirred frequently as it begins to brown. You may be sure that, if you leave it, it will burn. If you must answer the telephone, ladle about ⅓ cup (75 ml) of water into the pan to hold it back. After you hang up, continue cooking and stirring until the water has evaporated and the soffritto is the right color.

Learning to make a good soffritto takes time and patience. When you have made it many times, paying close attention to what you are doing and to how the soffritto behaves in different kinds of dishes, it will begin to become second nature to you, and you will be well on your way to understanding Tuscan cooking. The recipes in this book and in other Tuscan cookbooks will give you plenty of opportunities to practice.

Traditional Tuscan Cooking

This is not meant to be just a recipe book: *100 Quick and Easy Dishes Inspired by Sunny Tuscany*. Instead it is an introduction to the traditional cooking of my region. I offer my approach, as a Tuscan woman and a restaurateur, to preparing this cuisine in a contemporary way. This book is at least as much about my attitude toward food as it is a record of cooking procedures. I strongly believe it is impossible to cook well by just following recipes. Good cooking is an act of creativity. I have tried to give the most accurate descriptions and instructions that I can for preparing the dishes, but you must add something of your own. The recipes in this book are not meant to be followed like scientific formulas, full of precise details and step-by-step instructions. Use the recipes as indications, and trust your instincts to fill in the blanks. In doing so, you will develop a new level of authority in the kitchen.

I will try to show how dealing with food in a careful way, using all of the senses, can be more satisfying and restorative than we are accustomed to these days.

Unfortunately, for many years now, in Italy as throughout the world, the trend has been toward the maximum possible simplification of food and cooking, with the rationale that this meets the needs of modern life. Advertisements for food products tell us, in essence, "You have more important things to do; therefore we will supply you with a system that will enable you to be nourished merely by opening packages and pressing a few buttons." Now we can get vegetables already washed, peeled, cut, gassed, cooked, and frozen—small, cold corpses that, before such processing, were part of the chain of life.

All this has unavoidably brought about a distant and sterile relationship between people and their food. We have eliminated most preparation tasks, tasks that were our chance to become acquainted with food using the sensitive instruments we are lucky enough to have. Think for a moment about a freshly picked apple. Try to use all your senses to imagine the apple, and you will discover how closely they are interrelated. Together, they stimulate a potent desire to eat that apple. I believe it is imperative to sharpen our senses of sight, smell, touch, and taste before even speaking about cooking.

So I will start with the most basic recipes, so basic that they'll let me re-create on paper what I hope you will do in practice: trying the food, tasting and discussing it, enjoying it, and getting into its flavors. I mean to debunk the common myths that the more complex a dish is, the tastier it will be, and that the more difficult it is to prepare, the more skilled the cook must be.

The recipes in this chapter demonstrate that it is possible to eat fresh, home-cooked, warm, and delicious food without spending hours at the stove. It is possible to have friends to dinner without disrupting the usual routine of life and work. But please do not confuse simplicity with carelessness or superficiality: A simple dish should not be prepared with less care. On the contrary, the less complicated a dish is, the easier it will be to identify both its flaws and its virtues.

An ingredient you will never find in any cookbook is attention. For me, this is indispensable for a good outcome. By "attention" I do not mean just concentration, but also devotion to the thing you are doing. Your cooking will never come to its fruition without your full participation.

To put it simply, add to the recipe a pinch of love, select the finest and freshest ingredients, and don't let yourself worry if you are carried away by the flavors or tempted by your own appetite.

Sauces and Pasta

We begin with some traditional first courses, starting with a few recipes for fresh tomato sauce—often called *pomarola*. These sauces come first because they are extremely simple and because spaghetti with tomato sauce is the real national dish, the ubiquitous staple food, of Italy.

First, though, let me suggest that if you don't already have one, you acquire a simple, old-fashioned manual food mill. This is usually the best tool to use to strain and purée tomatoes and other cooked vegetables and fruits. While an electric food processor or a blender will also purée the food, it will not remove the seeds or bits of skin, and it will aerate the food in a way that can be undesirable. So, whenever a recipe calls for it, please use a food mill if you can. If a food processor or blender will do just as well, I will say so when I give the procedure.

An ingredient you will never find in any cookbook is attention. For me, this is indispensable for a good outcome.

♦

In the morning before Zibibbo opens, Armando picks herbs and tomatoes in the market garden across the street from the restaurant.

Pasta con pomarola

PASTA AND TOMATO SAUCE WITH GARLIC AND BASIL

Serves 4

3 tablespoons (50 ml) extra virgin olive oil

2 cloves garlic, coarsely chopped

1 pound (500 g) fresh or canned tomatoes, peeled and halved

Salt

½ teaspoon sugar (optional)

10 leaves basil, torn into large pieces

2 to 3 tablespoons (30 to 50 ml) extra virgin olive oil or unsalted butter, for dressing

½ teaspoon ground chile pepper (optional) (see Choosing Ingredients)

1 pound (500 g) dried pasta

1 cup (125 g) grated Parmesan cheese, for serving

Among the simplest sauces, and perhaps the best during the tomato season, is a very plain sauce made only with tomatoes, garlic, extra virgin olive oil, and basil. You need about a pound of fresh and fully ripe tomatoes, but in winter, they may be replaced by canned, peeled, whole tomatoes, preferably of the San Marzano variety. This sauce requires about 10 minutes to prepare, the time it takes to boil the pasta. Cook the pasta (see the instructions on page 15) while you are making the sauce, so that both will be ready at the same time. Simple tomato sauces like this one do not stick much to the pasta; therefore short pasta (penne rigate or farfalle, for example) is more suitable than spaghetti. In Italy, pasta dishes are served as first courses, without any accompaniment.

Put the oil and garlic in a pot over medium heat. Any type of pot will do, except earthenware, as it will maintain a high temperature for too long and will overcook the sauce. Stir the garlic as the oil heats, and as soon as you hear a sizzling sound, toss in the tomatoes. Do not allow the garlic to brown, because that would give a burnt flavor to the sauce. Add a little salt, and keep cooking for 6 to 7 minutes, until you see the tomatoes becoming soft. Strain the sauce through a food mill and taste it, both to adjust the salt and also because it might be slightly acidic, especially if you're using tomatoes that are not fully ripe or canned tomatoes. This may be corrected with a bit of sugar, perhaps half a teaspoon.

♦

Maria Roschi preserves her special Pomarola sauce in containers she has saved all year.

Put the strained sauce on the stove again over a medium flame and as soon as it starts boiling, add the basil and remove from the heat.

Ten minutes before you are ready to serve, start the pasta (see page 15). As soon as you drain it, while it is still very hot, dress it with the sauce. Once it cools it is no good. I suggest you mix in either oil or butter. Butter has a more delicate taste; if you prefer oil, a little ground red chile pepper will add some character. Freshly grated Parmesan cheese is a mandatory final addition to the dish, especially when butter is used.

Tomato sauces may be kept in the refrigerator, well-sealed, for up to 2 days, and gently reheated over low heat just before using.

VARIATION WITH FRESH TOMATOES AND PARSLEY
Serves 4

The second version of this recipe is slightly more elaborate, and I recommend using fresh tomatoes. These give better results if peeled first, so I am going to teach you how to do it.

Once and forever, I recommend that you wash all vegetables with the utmost care, but do not leave them immersed in water for any length of time, lest they lose flavor.

To peel the tomatoes, bring a pot of water to a boil; toss in the tomatoes, leaving them in the water for just a few seconds. Retrieve the tomatoes with a large slotted spoon and, as soon as you can handle them, rub them gently all along the surface with the blunt edge of a knife, then peel the loosened skin with your fingers.

In addition to the ingredients listed for the first version of this sauce, you will need:

1 tablespoon minced flat-leaf parsley
1 egg yolk (optional)
Freshly ground black pepper (optional)

Put the oil and garlic in a pot over medium heat. The pot should be rather large and shallow in this case, to enable the heat to reach most of the sauce at once. Stir the garlic as the oil heats, and as soon as you hear a sizzle, throw in the tomatoes and turn the heat up to high. Because this sauce will not be strained, you may squash the toma-toes with a fork at the bottom of the pot. Add salt sparingly. After 6 to 7 minutes, add the parsley and basil. Lower the heat to medium, and let the mixture cook for another 2 minutes, then take the pot off the stove.

This sauce also may be flavored with either oil or butter. If you prefer the latter, I suggest a variation to make the sauce tastier and better-blended: before adding it to the pasta, when it is still in the pan but no longer over the heat, add an egg yolk and a little black pepper.

Another little trick when using butter for dressing pasta: Melt it first. It is enough to keep the butter next to a source of heat, which may be the same pot in which you are boiling the pasta, or to toss it into the warm sauce.

Cooking Pasta

At this point, some considerations about how to cook pasta might be useful. The quality of the pasta is paramount. Buy brands made only of durum wheat (this should be clearly labeled—it is called *semola* in Italian), which withstands cooking much better than other varieties of wheat. Use abundant boiling water to which you must add salt, because once the pasta is cooked it cannot be salted anymore.

It is not merely better, or advisable, but imperative: *Pasta must be cooked al dente.* Overcooked pasta is muck, and there is no reason to punish your dining companions this way.

It takes some expertise to put perfectly cooked pasta on your dinner plates, but a general rule applies for all dried pasta: Use the directions on the package as a guide, stir the pasta occasionally, and taste it after 6 or 7 minutes. At this point, add more salt if you think the pasta needs it. Taste it again when you think the right moment is close, and drain it as soon as you find that the core is still firm but not hard. Bear in mind that from the time you drain it until it's eaten, the pasta continues cooking. Fresh pasta is cooked in the same way, but it requires only 1½ to 3 minutes of boiling.

The way you drain the pasta must suit the consistency of the sauce. If the sauce is very thick, the pasta has to be wetter so that the sauce will be a little more fluid; if the sauce is more liquid, the pasta should be drained thoroughly. Note that it may be better to retrieve fresh or dried egg noodles or tagliatelle (thin strips of fresh pasta) from the cooking water with a large fork rather than tossing it in a colander. This preserves the starch on the surface of the pasta, which would be leached away by the draining water, leaving the pasta gluey and lumpy.

CANNING POMAROLA TOMATOES

Peeling tomatoes is the first step for canning them, and for making tomato sauce for the winter, which used to be a widespread custom. It's not so popular nowadays, but well worth your while if you have an abundance of good, ripe tomatoes in season. If you want to try canning your tomatoes, boil glass canning jars and their flat lids to sterilize them. Fill the jars with peeled tomatoes, pressing them down as far as possible without rupturing them, and layering well-washed basil leaves in between them. Seal the jars with their sterilized flat lids and metal rings, then wrap each jar with a clean dish towel (or whatever other cloth you have). Immerse the jars in a large kettle filled with water up to the top of the jars, bring to a boil, and boil for about 10 minutes. Tomatoes and sauces canned this way last the whole winter, but once opened, the whole jar must be used at once and never put back in the refrigerator.

Pasta con pomarola con verdure
PASTA AND TOMATO SAUCE WITH VEGETABLES
Serves 6

1 pound (500 g) fresh or canned tomatoes, peeled

1 red onion, minced

1 carrot, peeled and coarsely chopped

1 stalk celery, minced

1 tablespoon minced flat-leaf parsley

1 clove garlic, minced

10 leaves basil

1 pound (500 g) dried pasta

½ cup (125 ml) extra virgin olive oil

½ teaspoon ground chile pepper (see Choosing Ingredients)

1 cup (125 g) grated Parmesan cheese, for serving

◆

Spaghetti dressed with Pomarola con verdure and Parmesan cheese

This sauce can be prepared in two ways. In either version, if you are using fresh tomatoes, cut them into large pieces; if canned, use them whole. These sauces are different from the basic tomato sauces, with their fresh, barely cooked tomatoes. In the basic sauces, the subtle and delicate flavors of tomato and basil are still distinct and recognizable; here, all the flavors are combined, producing the harmonic yet distinctive taste of a true sauce.

Combine the tomatoes, onion, carrot, celery, parsley, and garlic in a saucepan and cook over medium heat for about 15 minutes, stirring occasionally until the vegetables are tender.

While the sauce is cooking, start the pasta (see page 15). When the vegetables are cooked, purée them with a food mill and transfer the purée back to the saucepan. Put the sauce on the stove again for a couple of minutes over medium heat, then turn off the heat, stir in the basil, and the sauce is finished.

As soon as you drain the pasta, dress it with the sauce and then the oil. Serve immediately, while it is very hot. A little ground chile pepper will spice it up a bit, whether added while the sauce is cooking or when you dress the pasta.

This sauce and the version that follows do not require any more additional seasoning when you serve the pasta—except, of course, for a generous sprinkling of grated Parmesan cheese onto each serving.

VARIATION WITH LARDO

Serves 6

This second version uses the same ingredients and amounts as the first (except that in this case garlic and parsley are not required and the carrot should be minced, not chopped), but we add:

1½ ounces (40 g) lardo, diced (see Choosing Ingredients)
Salt

The procedure for this version is different and a little more elaborate. It starts with a soffritto, so combine the onion, carrot, celery, and oil in a pan over medium heat. For this sauce, the vegetables should not become too brown, but they must be fully cooked. Stir them frequently and watch them constantly. Add ⅓ cup (75 ml) of water, and when this is completely evaporated, the vegetables should continue cooking until they reach a light golden color. This will take 15 to 20 minutes. Toss in the tomatoes and squash them with a fork, then add the *lardo*. Cook for about 20 minutes over a medium heat, until the sauce has thickened. Add salt sparingly at first, then shortly before it's done add more salt as you like. Remove from the heat and stir in the basil.

After the pasta has been drained, dress it with the sauce. Serve immediately, while it is still very hot.

Soups and Broths

"Macaroni Italians"—a derogatory nickname formerly used to describe Italian immigrants in some countries—have exported spaghetti all over the world, making it an international food. Tired joke aside, the association between Italy and pasta is so ingrained into our consciousness that it's hard to believe that this food hasn't always existed. However, dried pasta as we know it did not appear until the beginning of the nineteenth century. As a matter of fact, Italian cooking has plentiful *primi*—first courses—of earlier origin, such as soups and broths. These have not become as popular as pasta, but they are at least as good.

In Tuscany, where the vegetable garden used to be the peasant's blessing, a large variety of vegetable-based soups used to be popular first courses. Two variations are described in the following recipes. Both use similar ingredients, but somewhat different procedures.

SIMPLE MINESTRONE

Serves 6

1 red onion, coarsely chopped

1 leek, white and tender green parts, coarsely chopped

2 carrots, peeled and coarsely chopped

2 stalks celery, coarsely chopped

1 or 2 boiling potatoes, peeled and coarsely chopped

3 zucchini (courgettes), coarsely chopped

1 clove garlic, sliced

2 fresh or canned tomatoes, peeled and coarsely chopped

Salt

2 small bunches of spinach, stemmed

15 leaves basil

2 cups (225 g) croutons, or 1 cup (225 g) cooked vialone nano rice (see Choosing Ingredients), or
*   1½ cup (240 g) ziti pasta (optional)*

⅓ cup (75 ml) extra virgin olive oil, for serving

This version of minestrone is a very mild vegetable purée, to be served with croutons, or rice (not *carnaroli*, the rice often used in risotto, but a shorter grain called *vialone nano*), or small pasta tubes, such as ziti, cooked separately. This is easy to make, and is very popular with small children. No doubt it is obvious to say it, but to obtain a tasty and fragrant vegetable purée, you must use the freshest vegetables, and cook them for the shortest possible time so that their flavor does not steam away.

Put the onion, leek, carrots, celery, potatoes, zucchini, garlic, and tomatoes in a soup pot with just enough salted water to come 1 inch (2 cm) below their level. Cover, bring to a boil, and cook until the vegetables are soft, about 20 minutes. Add the spinach and basil a few minutes before all the other vegetables are cooked. Strain the cooked vegetables through a food mill (or use a food processor). Return the mixture to the pot and add the rice or ziti, if using them. Ladle the soup into individual bowls and drizzle 1½ tablespoons of oil over each serving. If you are using croutons, serve them in a communal bowl and let guests sprinkle as few or as many as they like over their soup. You may serve the soup hot, though in summertime it is quite good served at room temperature. As with all first courses, it is served without any side dishes.

CLASSIC MINESTRONE
Serves 6

½ cup (125 ml) extra virgin olive oil

1 red onion, minced

2 stalks celery, 1 minced and 1 cubed

2 carrots, peeled, 1 minced and 1 cubed

1½ ounces (40 g) lardo, diced (optional) (see Choosing Ingredients)

¼ savoy cabbage, cut into small strips

1 or 2 boiling potatoes, peeled and cubed

3 zucchini (courgettes), cubed

2 fresh or canned tomatoes, peeled and cubed

1 clove garlic, sliced

About 2 cups (250 ml) meat stock (see page 24), or water

Salt

1½ cups (250 g) cooked white cannellini or navy beans, cooking liquid reserved (see page 106)

2 small bunches of spinach, stemmed and cut into thin strips

15 leaves basil

1½ cups (240 g) cooked ziti pasta (optional)

This second variation is richer and tastier, the famous Minestrone—to be written with a capital letter as a mark of respect. A little more time is needed for this version, along with some cabbage, some cannellini beans with their cooking water, and some meat stock. This classic minestrone starts with a soffritto, and the vegetables should be cut with more care than for the simple minestrone, as the soup will not be strained.

In a heavy-bottomed soup pot over medium heat, combine the oil, onion, minced celery, and minced carrot. Sauté, stirring frequently, until the soffritto is medium golden to light brown, about 15 minutes. Add the *lardo* when the soffritto is almost done and cook for a few minutes.

Put the cubed celery, cubed carrot, cabbage, potatoes, zucchini, tomatoes, and garlic into the pot with enough meat stock to come to a level 1 inch (2 cm) below the vegetables. Add a little salt and bring to a boil, stirring occasionally. After about 20 minutes, when the vegetables are tender, add the beans with about a cup of their cooking water and return the pot to a simmer for 3 to 4 minutes, then add the spinach and basil and cook for just 3 to

4 minutes more. As the soup cooks, taste to monitor both the saltiness and the vegetables' degree of doneness, taking care not to overcook them. You want them to be tender but not mushy.

This minestrone may be served with ziti cooked separately. Remove from heat, and stir in the ziti. Or, perhaps better, serve with no pasta.

◆

A produce vendor methodically shells cannellini beans in the market.

Zuppa lombarda
LOMBARD BEAN SOUP
Serves 8

2 pounds (1 kg) fresh white cannellini or navy beans, or 1 pound (500 g) dried

3 cloves garlic, 2 coarsely chopped and 1 whole

2 fresh or canned tomatoes, peeled and coarsely chopped

2 prosciutto rinds, coarsely chopped (see Choosing Ingredients)

8 to 10 leaves sage

6 (½-inch- or 1-cm-thick) slices Tuscan-style bread (see Choosing Ingredients)

1 cup (250 ml) extra virgin olive oil, for dressing

Freshly ground black pepper

This soup, despite its name, is a traditional Tuscan soup. It was the usual meal of the Lombard farmhands coming to the fields of Tuscany at wheat-threshing and grape-picking time. They were paid by the day and fed on beans. The basic ingredients are bread, garlic, oil, beans, and black pepper.

This soup is extremely simple, the only challenge being to find suitable bread. If it is not Tuscan it must be something very similar, that is, without fat, without salt, baked in loaves of about 2 pounds (1 kg) each, and preferably leavened with natural yeast. You can find similar large, round loaves of plain white bread under names such as boule, peasant, paesano Italian country, and the like, in your local bakery. Use fresh beans when they are in season, preferably the white variety we call cannellini.

Put the beans, along with the chopped garlic, tomatoes, prosciutto rinds, and sage leaves in a heavy (preferably earthenware) pot with enough water to cover by about 2 inches (5 cm). Simmer over a very low flame, without stirring, until the beans are fully cooked, about 40 to 50 minutes. If you're using dried beans, soak them overnight to soften them before cooking and increase the cooking time to at least 1 hour.

Toast the bread slices so that they become crisp on both sides. Rub the remaining garlic clove over both sides of the toasted bread. In order to most fully enjoy this soup, it is best to assemble it at the table. First put a slice of the bread in each of the dishes, then pour some beans, including some of the cooking water, over the bread. Dress each soup plate with 2 tablespoons of oil and add pepper. The bread should not soak in the broth for long; this would impair its texture and taste.

◆

Antonio Calvelli bakes twenty-five loaves of Tuscan bread every Saturday morning for his family and neighbors. While the bread is still hot from the oven, he brushes off the flour and ash from the bottom of each loaf.

Considering how often stock is mentioned

in our recipes, it is probably worthwhile

to learn how to make it yourself. Stock

is the liquid resulting from the cooking

of various foods in water. These may

be vegetables only, vegetables and meat,

or vegetables and fish. Don't let the fact

that it is liquid mislead you into believing

that it is a light food because, especially

if made with meat, it is quite substantial

as well as nutritious. In addition to

being an excellent first course in itself,

served with cappelletti (small tortellini)

or passatelli (see page 25), meat stock

is also an ingredient, sometimes

necessary, sometimes optional, in

many dishes.

◆

Benedetta squeezes the passatelli mixture

through a potato ricer before dropping it

into meat stock.

Bollito e Brodo
BOILED BEEF AND MEAT STOCK
Serves 6

2 red onions, peeled

2 stalks celery

2 carrots, peeled

2 fresh or canned tomatoes, peeled

A few leaves basil or 1 whole clove

1¼ pounds (800 g) whole beef shoulder

¼ stewing chicken

1 small joint of veal tail or oxtail

1 beef bone, any kind

Salt

In Tuscany, when a pot is put on the stove to make stock, a whole meal is in the making: usually a soup with small pasta cooked in the stock, boiled meat, and vegetables cooked separately. Moreover, Tuscan cooking, traditionally rich with imaginative ways for using leftovers, includes a long list of recipes whose main ingredient is the boiled meat left over from the previous day. Some of these recipes are so tasty that they are more appreciated than the original boiled meat. For the time being, let us try to just make a good meat stock to be used for many other things.

If you're cooking on a gas range, scorch the onions directly over an open flame for 2 minutes (you may also do this under a broiler). Then put them with all the other ingredients, including some salt, into a large stockpot. Fill the pot with enough cold water to cover the meat and vegetables by 2 inches (5 cm). Cook over low heat for a minimum of 2 hours, testing the various joints of meat with a fork from time to time. If you use a young chicken instead of a stewing hen or fowl (*gallina vecchia* in Italian), remove it from the pot earlier—it will be well done after 1 hour. When everything is cooked, remove the meat and bones with a large fork and strain the stock, discarding the vegetables, which will be nearly dissolved. If you intend to eat the boiled meat as such, reserve some stock to keep it warm until you serve it.

Passatelli

BREAD DUMPLINGS FOR MEAT BROTH

Serves 6

2¼ cups (300 g) dried bread crumbs
2¼ cups (300 g) grated Parmesan
   cheese plus 1 cup (125 g), for serving
6 eggs
1½ teaspoons grated nutmeg
Zest of 1 lemon, grated
6 cups (1½ l) meat stock (see page 24)
Freshly ground black pepper

This simple dish makes an excellent first course. In a large bowl, mix the bread crumbs, Parmesan, eggs, nutmeg, and lemon with your hands. Cover and let rest in the refrigerator for 1 hour.

Form the dough into balls the size of oranges. Bring the stock to a boil over medium heat. Put the balls through a potato ricer (using the large-holed disk) directly into the boiling stock. Serve, piping hot in soup bowls. Sprinkle a generous tablespoon of Parmesan and a bit of pepper over each serving.

Contorni: Vegetable Side Dishes

The variety of vegetables that a region produces is an indicator of its culinary tradition. Unfortunately, vegetables have become marginal in our way of eating. To many people, in fact, they seem to be regarded more as a punishment than as a source of pleasurable nourishment. They have disappeared from the menus of restaurants except as decorative elements, and they have vanished from the daily meal at home because they require too much preparation time. This is regrettable, because vegetables are the great wealth of a cuisine—particularly of Italian cooking, in which we find a huge variety of produce and an infinite number of ways to prepare it from region to region.

You will find many recipes for vegetable-based dishes throughout this book, not because I am anxious to promote a health food agenda, but because vegetables are so good. Their well-known nutritional value is just a bonus. In a formal meal, *contorni* are served with second, or main courses.

Pomodori gratinati
CRUSTY BAKED TOMATOES
Serves 6

Salt
6 fresh, very ripe tomatoes, cut in half lengthwise
3 tablespoons finely chopped flat-leaf parsley
3 tablespoons dried bread crumbs
½ cup (125 ml) extra virgin olive oil

For this recipe, it is absolutely necessary that the tomatoes, preferably of the San Marzano variety, be fresh, in season, and very ripe.

Salt the tomato halves and place them face down in a baking pan, letting them rest outside of the oven for about 15 minutes so that they lose a little water. Mix the parsley and bread crumbs together. Turn the tomatoes face up and sprinkle them with the mixture. Coat the pan with oil. Bake at 300°F (150°C) until the tomatoes are soft, about 20 to 30 minutes, basting them every so often with the cooking juices. Serve them on the same plate as a main course or as a side dish.

Zucchine trifolati
ZUCCHINI WITH GARLIC AND OREGANO
Serves 6

½ cup (125 ml) extra virgin olive oil

2 cloves garlic, sliced

12 small zucchini (courgettes), sliced about ½ inch (1 cm) thick

1½ teaspoons chopped fresh oregano, or ½ teaspoon dried

1½ teaspoons chopped fresh marjoram, or ½ teaspoon dried

Salt

This is an extremely simple and quick recipe. Only prepare it, though, if you have very fresh zucchini squash. No cooking liquid is required, so the zucchini must not have lost any of their own natural moisture. This is also why this dish is so delicious: The vegetable does not lose its flavor in water.

In an aluminum pot, combine the oil, garlic, zucchini, oregano, marjoram, and a pinch of salt. Keep it well covered and cook at a very low heat for about 10 minutes. Check the zucchini often and stir them with a wooden spoon while they're cooking to keep them from sticking to the bottom. Serve hot.

♦

San Marzano tomatoes
ready to bake for Pomodori gratinati.

Radicchio al forno
BAKED RED RADICCHIO
Serves 6

12 heads red radicchio

1 cup (250 ml) red wine

3 tablespoons (50 ml) extra virgin olive oil, plus more for dressing

Salt

Freshly ground black pepper

1 teaspoon (5 ml) freshly squeezed lemon juice, for dressing

This side dish has many fans, all with an affinity for its bitter taste. The best quality of red radicchio (chicory) for this recipe is called *trevigiano*, after Treviso, the town near Venice where they are grown. They may be recognized by their tapered, rather than rounded, shape. Allow two heads per person, because radicchio shrinks a lot while cooking. Wash each head thoroughly, discarding the external leaves and scraping the stem with a knife.

Lay the radicchio in a baking pan in a single layer. Pour the red wine and oil over them, then season with salt and pepper. Bake at 400°F (200°C) for 15 minutes, then take the pan out of the oven, turn all the radicchio over, add a little more salt, and put it back in the oven for another 20 minutes. Probe the radicchio stems with a fork to monitor cooking; the stems will be tender when they're done. Serve the dish hot, adding a little more oil and a few drops of lemon juice to each serving.

Fagiolini umido
BRAISED GREEN BEANS
Serves 4

◆

A vendor spills his beans
on a busy morning
at the Sant'Ambrogio market.

1 pound (500 g) green beans, trimmed
3 fresh or canned tomatoes, chopped
1 red onion, chopped
1 stalk celery, chopped
1 carrot, peeled and chopped
3 tablespoons (50 ml) extra virgin olive oil
½ cup (125 ml) water
Salt

This is a delicious side dish to accompany many meat courses. It is not demanding to prepare. The most boring and time-consuming operation is the cleaning of the green beans, which should not take more than ten minutes.

Put the beans, tomatoes, onion, celery, carrot, oil, water, and some salt in a small, uncovered pot over a medium flame. The beans take about 20 minutes to cook, but check them often, turning them gently with a wooden spoon. Do not overcook them! When the beans are ready they will still be firm, but just soft enough to pierce them with a fork. The water will be all but evaporated, and a light sauce will have formed. Serve warm.

Puré di patate
POTATO PURÉE

Serves 6

2 pounds (1 kg) boiling potatoes
2 cups (500 ml) milk
Salt
7 tablespoons (100 g) unsalted butter
2 cups (250 g) grated Parmesan cheese

In Tuscany, this purée, although made of potatoes, is considered a formal side dish. It is essentially mashed potatoes lavishly enriched with a lot of butter and Parmesan cheese, and it is usually served with substantial meat courses, roasts, or stews. The dish looks simple, but it is not; it requires a lot of care and some practice to get the right consistency. It is essential that all ingredients are added when the purée is hot, otherwise it will never be smooth enough. You may need to practice making it several times, critically examining the results, before you feel you have mastered it. Note that the quantities given should be taken as approximate, as they vary considerably with the potato quality.

Wash the potatoes, put them in a pot of cold water, and boil for about 20 minutes, probing them from time to time with a fork. Once you are satisfied that the potatoes are cooked inside, drain them, and peel them as soon as they are cool enough to handle. Heat the milk in a small pan, taking care not to boil it. Pour half of the warm milk into a pot large enough to hold the potatoes. Reserve the remaining milk, keeping it warm over a very low flame—again, be careful not to scorch it. Put the potatoes through a food mill directly into the pot of warm milk. Set the pot on a very low flame and stir continuously with a wooden spoon for about 5 minutes. Add salt to taste.

A good potato purée must not be too thick, so add more milk, continuing to stir, until you think the purée is the right consistency. Taste for salt, then add the butter and Parmesan. Take the pot off the stove and keep stirring until the butter has melted and mixed in well. Should you need to reheat the purée, put it in a bain-marie or double boiler over low heat, always stirring it with a wooden spoon. Serve hot.

♦

Local grapes, pears, and peaches
are carefully presented
at the Sant'Ambrogio market.

Main Courses

Next are five fish dishes, all very simple and quick. Each is ideal as a main course, but they may be moved around the menu as you wish. May I also point out the lightness and digestibility of the following recipes? This is a strategy of mine to tempt you.

Insalata di gamberi e sedano
SHRIMP, CELERY, AND TOMATO SALAD
Serves 6

1 pound (500 g) large shrimp (prawns)

1 bunch celery

2 whole scallions (spring onions), sliced in rounds

1 clove garlic, minced

2 fresh, very ripe tomatoes, seeded and diced

1 tablespoon chopped fresh oregano, or 1 teaspoon dried

2 tablespoons chopped flat-leaf parsley

½ cup (125 ml) extra virgin olive oil

Juice of 1 lemon

Salt

¼ teaspoon ground chile pepper (see Choosing Ingredients)

This cold dish is very pleasant in summer. I would not want to define it as a true and proper second course, but it is a salad that you can insert in the menu wherever it pleases you.

In a small pot, boil enough salted water to cover the shrimp. Put the shrimp in the water for 2 minutes, then drain them and let them chill in the air until they're cool enough to handle, then shell and devein them. Remove the greenest and hardest stalks from the bunch of celery and wash the remaining stalks well before slicing them finely. Place the celery with the shrimp in a serving bowl, and add the scallions, garlic, tomatoes, oregano, and parsley.

Just before you're ready to serve the salad, dress it with the oil, lemon juice, salt, and ground chile. If the salad sits in its dressing waiting to be eaten, the salt will make the green vegetables lose their liquid and the salad will become watery.

Zuppa di frutti di mare

SHELLFISH SOUP

Serves 6

6½ pounds (3 kg) assorted shellfish, such as mussels, cherrystone clams, and small crabs

3 cloves garlic, 2 minced and 1 whole

2 tablespoons minced flat-leaf parsley

1 fresh chile pepper, minced (see Choosing Ingredients)

⅓ cup (75 ml) extra virgin olive oil

4 fresh or canned tomatoes, peeled

1½ teaspoons chopped fresh oregano, or ½ teaspoon dried

1½ teaspoons chopped fresh marjoram, or ½ teaspoon dried

Salt

1 lemon, quartered

½ cup (125 ml) white wine

Tuscan-style bread, sliced and toasted, for serving (see Choosing Ingredients)

As well as a main course, this dish can also be served as a first course. Scrub the shell-fish, rinsing them several times. Thoroughly clean the outsides of the mussels with a knife, tearing away the beards protruding from the shells.

Combine the garlic, parsley, and chile pepper with the oil in a stockpot large enough to contain the whole soup. Put the pot over medium heat, stirring as the oil heats so the garlic does not burn. As soon as the oil begins to sizzle, add the tomatoes and squash them with a fork. When the tomato juice starts to bubble, add the oregano and marjoram, and just enough salt to season the tomatoes. Simmer briefly, 2 to 3 min-utes, before adding the seafood, lemon, and wine. Stir with a wooden spoon and cover tightly. Cook for 5 to 7 minutes over a medium-low heat, stirring every now and then to ensure the seafood cooks evenly. When all the shells are open and the crab is pink, the soup is done; take the pot promptly off the stove. Serve the soup piping hot, accom-panied with slices of toasted bread rubbed with a peeled clove of garlic to soak up the tasty liquid.

A note about etiquette: Despite what you may have been taught, crabs, shellfish, and crustaceans in general should be eaten with the hands, using the empty shells as spoons to pick up a little sauce.

◆

Telline and date clams

Spiedini di pescatrice e gamberi
BAKED MONKFISH, ASSORTED BELL PEPPERS, AND SHRIMP ON SKEWERS
Serves 6

24 extra-large shrimp (prawns), shelled and deveined

1 pound (500 g) monkfish fillets, membrane removed and cut in 1-inch (2-cm) pieces

1 yellow bell pepper (capsicum), seeded and cut in 1-inch (2-cm) squares

1 green bell pepper (capsicum), seeded and cut in 1-inch (2-cm) squares

1 red bell pepper (capsicum), seeded and cut in 1-inch (2-cm) squares

Salt

½ cup (125 ml) white wine

2 tablespoons (30 ml) extra virgin olive oil

1 tablespoon chopped fresh oregano, or 1 teaspoon dried

This dish, besides being good, has the merit of being very attractive and decorative for a buffet, since it can also be served cold. It works as either a main course or an appetizer.

Thread the seafood and peppers onto small skewers (about 6 inches or 15 cm long and fairly thin), beginning with a piece of pepper and alternating shrimp and fish with the various colors of peppers. Place the skewers in a baking pan and salt them, first on one side and then the other. Pour the wine and oil in the pan and sprinkle the oregano over the skewers. Bake at 300°F (150°C) for about 15 minutes, turning the skewers over halfway through the cooking time and basting them from time to time with their cooking juices. The fish are done when the flesh is completely white and showing no pink. Serve on skewers, one or two per person.

Calamari alla livornese
SQUID SAUTÉED IN TOMATO SAUCE
Serves 4

3 cloves garlic, minced

2 tablespoons minced flat-leaf parsley

1 fresh chile pepper, minced (see Choosing Ingredients)

½ cup (125 ml) extra virgin olive oil

1 pound (500 g) fresh or canned tomatoes, peeled
Salt
1¾ pounds (800 g) squid, cleaned and cut in ½-inch (1-cm) rings
Tuscan-style bread, sliced and toasted, for serving (see Choosing Ingredients)

This is the classic way of cooking squid (and other seafood) in the Tuscan port city of Livorno. The signature ingredients of this style are tomatoes, garlic, and parsley. This dish requires little time, little work, and little money. Serve it as a main course.

Put the garlic, parsley, chile pepper, and oil in a heavy-bottomed skillet over medium heat, stirring so the garlic doesn't burn as the oil heats. As soon as the oil starts sizzling, toss in the tomatoes and squash them with a fork. Let the tomatoes cook for about 5 minutes until the juice starts to bubble. Add a little salt, and when the tomato juice begins to thicken after about 2 more minutes, add the squid. Cook for no more than 10 minutes, turning the squid frequently. Taste for salt. Ladle into individual bowls and serve hot with toasted bread.

◆

At the Viareggio fish market, a lottery determines who the first fisherman will be to auction off his catch.

Filletti di sogliole fritti
FRIED FILLETS OF SOLE WITH LEMON AND GARLIC
Serves 6

12 fillets of sole

Salt

Freshly ground black pepper

2 cloves garlic, minced

2 tablespoons minced flat-leaf parsley

2 or 3 tablespoons all-purpose (plain) flour

1 egg

⅓ cup (30 g) dried bread crumbs

About 2 cups (500 ml) extra virgin olive oil

1 teaspoon (5 ml) freshly squeezed lemon juice

•

At Viareggio harbor,
a fleet of fishing boats wait out
a summer storm
as it darkens the western sky.

This is a very simple dish, if the difficulty of filleting the sole is excluded—a task best left to your trusted fishmonger. Mediterranean sole is the ideal fish for this preparation. Of the several varieties of sole (really flounder) available in North America, several are too flaky to fry up well. Ask your fishmonger for a lean, dense-fleshed sole, like English sole, petrale sole, or lemon sole, for the best results. This main dish is very agreeably accompanied by spinach blanched in salted boiling water and seasoned simply with good olive oil and a little lemon.

Spread the fillets on a cutting board and season them with salt, a little pepper, and pinches of the garlic and parsley. Starting from the top, roll up the fillets as tightly as you can, then roll them in the flour and set them aside for a moment. Beat the egg with a pinch of salt. Dip the rolled-up fillets in the egg, then roll them in the bread crumbs.

Choose a frying pan wide enough to accommodate all the fillets at once, and cover the bottom with 1 inch (2 cm) of oil. Heat over a high flame. The oil is ready when a bread crumb dropped in it sizzles. Fry the fillets for about 3 minutes, then turn them over and fry for another 2 to 3 minutes on the other side. The fillets should be browned well on both sides. Remove the fillets from the oil and drain them very briefly on absorbent paper, then serve immediately. Once fried, the fillets should be eaten very hot, sprinkled with a few drops of lemon juice.

Aroma
and
Taste

aroma and taste

As I walk about Florence, every now and then I happen to pass a kitchen that emits such a wonderful aroma that I have to stop for a while, inhaling as deeply as my lungs are able, trying to capture as much as I can. At such times, I wish I had a container in which to store that fragrance. I realize, though, that even if I stay there, close to the source, it will soon disappear. As more air passes beneath my nose, the aroma will dissipate, carrying with it the deep pleasure of that first sensation. Pity! When will I again come across another kitchen that smells so wonderful?

Aromas gently hover in the memory. Unfortunately, there is no way to file olfactory sensations and recall them at will, but when we do happen to come across them again, those first encounters come flooding back, with their surroundings, visual images, and sensations surprisingly complete.

I could write my life history as a series of olfactory memories. In one especially vivid flashback to my childhood, I recall how we used to go to my grandparents' big house in the country every year. I see myself as in a film, in heavy stockings and pleated skirt, rummaging through musty old trunks, or standing beside my grandmother, who is basting, with a pungent rosemary twig, the leg of lamb slowly turning in front of the hearth.

And you? Forget the present for a while, and think of the scents of past places and circumstances: the smell of a baby's room—a mixture of milk, rash-soothing ointments, plastic toys, and mother's love; of a primary school—glue, pencils, and erasers, and the stale lunch forgotten at the bottom of someone's knapsack; the smell of one's house after a few days away; of the church; of the stable; and of so many kitchens where you have been—kitchens that both attract you and promise you pleasures to come. Since my early childhood, the nose, rather than the mouth, has been the organ responsible for my passions; the wisp of steam coming from the pot is as long as my whole life.

◆

Marzapan fruits entice shoppers in Piazza San Giovanni. (above)

◆

The aroma of Roberto's freshly roasted chestnuts wafts through the streets of central Florence. (left)

Nowadays, we generally understand what is going on around us by using our eyes and ears. Our senses of smell and of taste were more important a long time ago, when humans needed them daily to sort out what was good to eat from what was not. But although our survival no longer depends so much on our ability to smell, our perception of aromas still connects us with our environment in a direct way. To capture a certain smell is like catching something real, getting closer to the physical world in a different way; it stirs that part of ourselves in which emotions are at a premium over rational thoughts.

I like to think that our senses of smell and taste have developed through the millennia to permit us not only to distinguish between good and bad, but also to increase our pleasure. This pleasure doesn't just exist for itself, but helps keep our lives in harmony. In short, I am firmly convinced that eating is not meant only for nourishment, but is and must be a pleasure.

We seldom try to interpret the messages coming in through our senses of taste and smell. Few are able to recognize odors blind, and the same applies to tastes. We also restrict our range of known and accepted tastes. Children, for example, seem to prefer only the most basic tastes and are totally unable to recognize and enjoy flavors that their young memories have not yet encountered.

If the hypothetical nourishment pill of science fiction is not so far away, it is not only because our food is becoming more like plastic, but also because we refuse to be inquisitive, we blunt the development of new tastes, and we reject food's pleasure-giving potential or consider it only as preventive medicine.

This part of the book is intended to illuminate the knowledge and pleasure we gain from smelling and tasting. The recipes are characterized by their emphasis on flavor—either a harmonic combination of flavors or the dominant notes of one or two ingredients. Here you will find recipes you can use to test the combination of contrasting tastes, and others in which the flavor combination is meant to enhance a particular taste.

♦

A couple shares gelato with their child.
(above)

♦

Pistachio nuts and prickly pear cactus
fruits flavor the gelato and granita
of Gelateria Carabè. (right)

Scents

In Italy, fresh herbs are called *odori* (which means "scents"). Following an old tradition, our greengrocers will offer you a small bunch of *odori* when you pay for your purchases. Before beginning with the recipes, let us imagine we have a small bunch of *odori*: basil, parsley, sage, thyme, celery, oregano, and a bay leaf. Let us take a leaf of each, crush it in our fingers, and smell it. What is it like? It is not so easy to describe it—when you sniff a basil leaf you can only think that it smells of basil. You could say, "It is sharp," but what herb is not? Perhaps the best way to compare our *odori* is to smell them in sequence.

Basil's scent begins almost pungent, then mellows into a simple plant essence, while parsley is plainer, less sharp, and less persistent, so that your fingers only retain a vegetable smell. What about sage? Sage, the feminine word *salvia* in Italian, is rich, overpowering, exciting, and certainly female. Thyme is intriguing, insinuating, tasty, and exciting, like a twenty-seven-year-old Parisian man. Celery, by contrast, is austere and sumptuous; it gives itself up slowly, and only if our intentions are serious. Oregano is aggressive enough to warn of the risk you may expose yourself to if you overdo it with lust. Finally, the bay leaf, being a descendant of the noble laurel, is serious and strict, like a gentleman wearing a jacket and silk scarf at home. Bay has some sharp points, but it gives its majestic scent to your nostrils without bewildering.

This tour of a bundle of *odori* is sheer fancy, but it is in tune with my purpose: to urge you to smell your ingredients and your dishes, to find in your memory the recollection you have of aromas, and to reflect on the sensations both new and remembered scents provoke.

Market vendors often present a gift of Odori to their customers.

Tastes

Another way to train your senses of smell and taste is to learn the differences in flavor, color, sharpness, and freshness between varieties of herbs. For example, wild rosemary growing near the sea has a much stronger flavor than the cultivated kind. Basil is available nowadays anywhere and any time, but what a difference between the fleshy green leaves of the plant growing in a pot in the full summer sun and the pale, rickety leaflets of greenhouse basil, which wilt at a glance! Small parsley is much tastier than the big one, and the same applies to celery. Indeed, in Tuscany there is a variety of celery to be used as *odori* as well as the one to be eaten as a vegetable.

The first three recipes are chosen as basic examples of how to link taste and aroma. The first one has a basic taste—mussels, prepared with white wine, lemon juice, and a bit of parsley. The second adds garlic, oregano, and marjoram, and in the third the herbs, amalgamated while cooking with the base ingredient (eggplant), play the role of flavor enhancers.

Gran piatto di cozze
GREAT PLATTER OF MUSSELS
Serves 6

2 pounds (1 kg) mussels, scrubbed and debearded

⅓ cup (75 ml) dry white wine

Salt

⅓ cup (75 ml) extra virgin olive oil, for dressing

1 tablespoon (15 ml) freshly squeezed lemon juice, for dressing

1 tablespoon minced flat-leaf parsley, for garnish

The name of this dish does not allude to its majesty, but rather to the fact that you will need a decidedly large platter to serve it. It is, however, a superb dish. If at all possible, I suggest you eat it in the summer as an appetizer, perhaps while you're on vacation near the sea. It is not foolish to consider where and when you eat something—this is part of the pleasure of tasting dishes. However, I don't think that it would occur to anyone to eat mussels in December in a mountain hut after skiing, nor to eat oxtail soup with dumplings in July on the Amalfi Coast.

In this recipe, it is truly essential that the mussels be of high quality: alive, of small size, and very flavorful. Put the mussels in a large pot with the wine and a little salt; cover tightly with a lid, and place over high heat. Cook for 5 to 7 minutes, until they have all opened. Take the mussels out of the pot, discarding any that haven't opened. When they are cool enough to handle, remove half of the shell from each mussel. Arrange the mussels on the half-shells on a tray. Season by drizzling a thin stream of oil and a few drops of lemon juice on each, sprinkle the parsley over them, and serve.

Note that when you use raw parsley as a seasoning, as in this recipe, it is important to wash it very well, then dry it with a clean cloth; you will not be able to mince it if it remains wet.

Insalata di cozze
MUSSEL AND TOMATO SALAD WITH GARLIC AND FRESH HERBS
Serves 6

3 pounds (1½ kg) mussels, scrubbed and debearded
⅓ cup (75 ml) dry white wine
1 clove garlic, finely chopped
Pinch of chopped fresh oregano
Pinch of chopped fresh marjoram
Pinch of chopped flat-leaf parsley
1 fresh tomato, chopped and seeded
Juice of 1 lemon
½ teaspoon chopped fresh chile pepper (optional) (see Choosing Ingredients)
Salt
⅓ cup (75 ml) extra virgin olive oil, for dressing
Tuscan-style bread, for serving (see Choosing Ingredients)

In the old days, folks promenading along the Tyrrhenian seashore in the evening could stop at a stand where the shellfish vendor would open, then and there, some ten raw mussels, sprinkle them with a little lemon, and give them to you on a saucer, ready to be eaten with the fingers and with a less than refined slurping noise. This is no longer possible; today mussels carry no health insurance, and therefore you must cook them. Serve this dish as an appetizer or simple first course.

Put the mussels and wine in a broad-bottomed pot over high heat and cover tightly. Cook until the mussels have steamed open, 5 to 7 minutes. Drain the mussels, discarding any that haven't opened, and shell them as soon as they're cool enough to handle.

Place the mussels in a serving bowl and add the garlic, oregano, marjoram, parsley, tomato, lemon juice, and—for those who like it—the chile pepper. Mix well, and taste to see if the mussels need any salt—often, they are salty enough. At the very end, add the oil. Don't put it in earlier, because it will coat the mussels, preventing them from absorbing the other flavors. Serve the mussels in individual bowls with small slices of untoasted Tuscan-style bread.

A common note for the two recipes above, where the tastes will coalesce only in the mouth, is that the balance among the flavors is paramount. Therefore, add ingredients with a light hand and adjust seasonings only as your taste indicates.

Melanzane appassite in forno
BRAISED EGGPLANT ROUNDS WITH GARLIC AND OREGANO
Serves 6

6 long, thin eggplants (aubergines), cut into 3-inch- or 6-cm-thick rounds

2 cloves garlic, slivered

2 teaspoons chopped fresh oregano

6 tablespoons (100 ml) red wine vinegar

3 tablespoons (50 ml) extra virgin olive oil, plus more for dressing

Salt

Freshly ground black pepper

In this dish, cooking truly melds the flavors. The taste of eggplant is amenable to an endless variety of more or less complicated flavor combinations, but in this instance, only a few ingredients will be added. Use the elongated Italian-style eggplants if you can find them, or else try the Japanese or Chinese varieties. This recipe may be served as an appetizer or as a side dish with the main course.

In a baking dish, place the eggplant rounds in a single layer. Into the top of each eggplant round, push a sliver of garlic and a few leaflets of oregano, taking care that they stick into the eggplant flesh. Pour the vinegar and oil evenly over the rounds, sprinkle with some salt, and cover the pan with aluminum foil. Bake at 375°F (190°C) for 20 minutes, then remove the foil and continue cooking uncovered for another 10 to 15 minutes, until the eggplant rounds are soft. Take them out of the oven, allowing them to cool a bit before placing them on a serving dish. Trickle on a little more oil, and add a pinch of pepper. This dish should not be served hot; serve it at room temperature or, in the summer, cold.

◆

Now that you've had an introduction to connecting aroma and taste in the three recipes above, it's time to venture out on your own and try the following recipes, bearing in mind the pleasure-giving powers of linking aroma and taste.

Minestrone alla genovese
GENOESE VEGETABLE SOUP WITH PESTO
Serves 8

⅓ cup (75 ml) extra virgin olive oil, plus more for serving

1 red onion, minced

3 carrots, peeled, 1 minced and 2 chopped

2 stalks celery, 1 minced and 1 sliced

¼ head savoy cabbage, cut in thin strips

2 leeks, white and tender green parts, sliced

2 zucchini (courgettes), cubed

3 large boiling potatoes, peeled and cubed

*1½ cups (250 g) cooked white cannellini
  or navy beans (see page 106)*

Salt

1½ cups pesto (see page 49), for serving

1 cup (125 g) grated Parmesan cheese, for serving

In the first chapter I described minestrone, but this recipe is not the one for the traditional minestrone made in Genoa, but for one that I particularly like. Every Ligurian town and village, and almost every family, has its own variation, so a standard recipe really doesn't exist. However, they are all good. Basically, this recipe is a vegetable soup to which pesto (basil sauce) is added before serving. Serve it as a first course.

First, make a soffritto. In a large aluminum stockpot, heat the oil over a medium flame. Add the onion, minced carrot, and minced celery and sauté until the vegetables are a light golden color, about 10 minutes. When the soffritto is done, add the chopped carrots, sliced celery, cabbage, leeks, zucchini, potatoes, and beans. Cover the ingredients with water, and add a little salt. Cover the pot, turn the heat down to very low, and cook for 25 to 30 minutes. Beginning after 20 minutes of cooking, stir periodically with a wooden spoon and check for doneness. When it is ready, the vegetables will be soft but not mushy.

Check for seasoning and adjust as necessary, then strain half the soup through a food mill (or, if you don't have a food mill, purée it in a food processor). Add the puréed soup back to the other half, finally adding the pesto.

This summertime soup should be served lukewarm with grated Parmesan cheese and a drizzle of oil forming a letter "C" in each dish.

◆

Basil

PESTO
Makes 1½ cups (375 ml)

2 cloves garlic, chopped
¼ cup (100 g) pine nuts
Salt
Leaves from 1 bunch basil, about ¼ pound (100 g), well washed and dried
½ cup (125 ml) extra virgin olive oil
1 cup (125 g) grated Parmesan cheese
½ cup (65 g) grated hard pecorino cheese (see Choosing Ingredients)

The famous pesto is an uncooked sauce featuring basil. I wish some skilled novelist would devote a few pages to describing it as an example of the subtle and harmonic relationship between Italian cooking, the land, and the culture of the inhabitants of so many different regions.

The pesto itself represents Liguria, carrying with it the breeze rising over salty seas; the shimmering of sunlight among tree branches, teasing the eyes; a hot summer on a terrace atop a rugged coastal cliff; the glitter of the sea; a beautifully laid table; light white wine; and the fragrance of sweet verbena mixed with scented geranium.

Because of this I am upset when I see plastic tubs of pesto lined up on the shelves of a supermarket. The contents are like a nourishment pill with a vague scent of basil. Please, make your own pesto. Even if you are on the thirty-second floor of a Manhattan skyscraper, while you are thinking of your pesto, selecting the ingredients, preparing it (it takes ten minutes), and tasting it, you will be re-creating a little bit of Liguria.

The basil for the pesto must be the kind grown in open air; it is easily recognized because its leaves, although thin, are strong and fleshy compared to the flimsy leaves of greenhouse basil.

♦

Pecorino and other cheeses on display at Fattoria Corzano & Paterno

No knives or other blades should be used for this sauce because they would alter the delicate flavor of the basil. The main ingredients—basil, garlic, nuts, and cheese—should be pounded into a paste with a pestle in a mortar (pesto in Italian means "pounded"). This operation is not so simple and it takes time. Many Italians nowadays use a hand-held food processor, which is not correct, but it makes things much easier.

If using a food processor, put the garlic, pine nuts, a pinch of salt, the basil, and the oil into the bowl and process until the ingredients form a smooth paste. Add the Parmesan and the pecorino and pulse just to combine. Taste and adjust the salt.

If making the pesto by hand, combine the garlic, pine nuts, a pinch of salt, and the basil in a mortar and pound the ingredients with a pestle until they have formed a paste. Add the cheeses and mix them into the pesto with a wooden spoon. Pour in the oil slowly, mixing it into the pesto until the sauce is smooth and creamy. Pesto can be safely kept in the refrigerator for up to 2 days, no longer.

Linguine al pesto
LINGUINI WITH PESTO SAUCE AND POTATO
Serves 6

1 pound (500 g) fresh or dried linguini
1 boiling potato, peeled and cubed
1 cup pesto (see page 49)
3 tablespoons (50 g) unsalted butter
1 cup (125 g) grated Parmesan cheese, for serving
Freshly ground black pepper, for serving

There is little to add in this recipe, besides a few hints about cooking the pasta (see page 15). Like all pasta dishes, this is a first course.

When cooking the pasta, add a potato to the salted water. This trick returns to the pasta the starch it tends to lose in draining, thus preventing the linguini from clumping. Drain the potato cubes along with the pasta, reserving a little of the cooking water. Transfer the pasta and potato to a large bowl and dress them with the pesto and butter. If the pasta looks too dry, add a little of the reserved cooking water. Serve in individual dishes, topping each with grated Parmesan cheese and pepper.

Tagliolini alle erbe
TAGLIOLINI WITH LEMON, BASIL, OREGANO, AND MARJORAM
Serves 6

2 large strips lemon zest

1 clove garlic, peeled

20 leaves basil

1 tablespoon chopped flat-leaf parsley

1½ teaspoons chopped fresh oregano, or ½ teaspoon dried

1½ teaspoons chopped fresh marjoram, or ½ teaspoon dried

Salt

1 pound (500 g) fresh tagliolini

⅓ cup (75 ml) extra virgin olive oil, for dressing

Some herbs, such as sage, rosemary, and bay leaves, can withstand long cooking. For this recipe, however, the dressing is to be prepared raw, in order to preserve as much as possible the flavor of these more delicate herbs. The choice of the pasta, tagliolini (flat, thin fresh noodles), is also meant to keep the taste of the pasta from overwhelming the flavors of the dressing. Serve as a first course.

Chop together the lemon zest and garlic, then add the basil, parsley, oregano, and marjoram. Keep on mincing until the mixture looks uniform. The amount of herbs is hard to determine, but for six people, the chopped mixture should fill an espresso cup; no more than that.

Meanwhile, cook the tagliolini in boiling salted water. (See suggestions for cooking fresh pasta on page 15.) When it is done, transfer to a bowl with a large fork, rather than draining it through a colander, which would cause it to clump together. Sprinkle the herb mixture onto the pasta, dress with the oil, toss, and serve immediately.

Spaghetti con uova di pesce
SPAGHETTI WITH A ROE, TOMATO, AND CHILE PEPPER SAUCE
Serves 6

⅔ cup (150 ml) extra virgin olive oil

2 cloves garlic, minced

1 or 2 fresh red chile peppers, chopped

2 or 3 fish roes from whitefish, sea bass, or golden bream

1 tablespoon minced flat-leaf parsley

1 fresh or canned tomato, peeled and cubed

Salt (optional)

1 pound (500 g) fresh or dried spaghetti

⅓ cup (75 ml) fish stock, or reserved pasta cooking water

♦

Zibbibo chefs can pick and choose from a bowl of chile peppers sitting on the serving counter.

I find this spaghetti superb, especially if eaten on a hot summer day. Apart from the difficulty of finding really fresh fish eggs—the best ones being those of whitefish, sea bass, or golden bream—the preparation is exceedingly simple. Don't worry if you have never cooked with roes before, they do not require washing or any special handling. Serve this dish as a first course.

Heat half of the oil in a pan with the garlic and chile peppers over a low flame. When the oil is hot, but before it sizzles, open the membranes containing the fish eggs with a sharp knife and let the roes fall into the pan. Gently scrape the membrane with the side of a fork to dislodge all the roe. Allow the roe to simmer for no more than 1 minute, stirring gently with a wooden spoon just enough to separate them. Take the pan off the stove and add the parsley and the tomato. This sauce will likely be salty enough without the addition of salt. Check it anyway, and if necessary, add salt to the pasta cooking water.

Meanwhile, cook the pasta al dente (see page 15). When draining the pasta, reserve some of the cooking water in case the drained pasta becomes too dry. If you happen to have some fish stock, use that to moisten the pasta, but the cooking water will also do.

Gently mix the drained pasta, the remaining ⅓ cup (75 ml) of oil, and the sauce in a serving bowl, adding a little fish stock or cooking water if required, until the pasta is thoroughly coated with the sauce. Serve hot, immediately.

Carpaccio di pesce spada con zenzero
SWORDFISH CARPACCIO WITH FRESH GINGER
Serves 6

1 pound (500 g) swordfish, sliced as thinly as possible

Salt

Juice of 1 lemon

2 tablespoons minced flat-leaf parsley

2 tablespoons (30 ml) extra virgin olive oil

1 teaspoon grated fresh ginger

Spread the slices of swordfish on serving plates and season each slice with a little salt, a few drops of lemon juice, and the parsley, oil, and ginger. This dish must be eaten as soon as it is seasoned, because if the fish marinates in the lemon its flavor changes completely. Serve as either an appetizer or a main course.

Tartara di orata
GILTHEAD TARTARE WITH LEMON MUSTARD DRESSING
SERVED WITH GREEN BEAN SALAD
Serves 4

1 pound (500 g) green beans, stemmed

1 clove garlic, minced

Juice of 1 or 2 lemons

¼ cup (60 ml), plus 3 tablespoons (50 ml) extra virgin olive oil

Seeds of 1 pomegranate (optional)

About 1½ pounds (650 g) gilthead fillets, or other fish

½ teaspoon (3 ml) strong prepared mustard

Salt

Freshly ground black pepper

In this dish the ingredients are not cooked at all. It is exquisite, though it can be terribly expensive—a folly for only every now and then or a special occasion. Use very fresh

♦

Fishermen unload their morning catch
of red mullet and mackerel
from Viareggio Bay.

gilthead seabream (*Sparus aurata*) if you live near the Eastern Atlantic or the Mediterranean. In the Americas or elsewhere in the world, try this with sea bass, striped bass, or the fish variously called dorado, dolphinfish, or mahimahi. Serve as a main course.

In a mixing bowl, toss together the green beans, garlic, 1 tablespoon (15 ml) of the lemon juice, the 3 tablespoons (50 ml) of oil, and the pomegranate seeds. Cut the fish with a sharp knife, first into thin strips and then into the smallest possible cubes, the size of a kernel of corn.

In a small bowl, dissolve the mustard in the remaining lemon juice. Add a pinch of salt and a little pepper. Mix in the fish and add the ¼ cup (60 ml) oil. Taste, check the salt, and serve immediately, accompanied by the green bean salad.

As in Carpaccio di pesce spada

con zenzero (see page 54), a lot of food

in this chapter is used raw, or just blanched.

In some cases, a raw ingredient is added

to something cooked. At the beginning

of this chapter., I discussed the virtues

of working with unaltered flavors and

tastes. One of the trends of "modern"

cooking is not to cook foods, or at least

to cook them as little as possible, in order

to avoid significant changes to the original

taste. This can be very good in some

instances, but cannot be considered real

cooking, notwithstanding what some famous

chefs may have recently claimed.

Braciole fritte con salse

VEAL CUTLETS WITH RAW TOMATO SAUCE OR ANCHOVY SAUCE

Serves 4

1 cup (250 ml) Raw Tomato Sauce (see page 57) or
½ cup (125 ml) Anchovy Sauce (see page 57)
1 pound (500 g) girello (veal top round)
1 large egg
Salt
1 cup (100 g) dried bread crumbs
Extra virgin olive oil, for frying

This is a way to serve fried food to guests without the need for the cook to leave the table during the meal and tend to the frying. Ideal for summertime, the best results are achieved by using round and regular slices of veal *girello,* the upper part of the leg, which is more tender and delicate when fried than other cuts. A green salad and string beans are both good accompaniments.

Choose one of the two sauces to prepare, either a tomato or an anchovy sauce. Prepare whichever sauce you prefer first, so it will be ready to serve when the meat is ready.

Cut the veal into slices about ½ inch (1 cm) thick. The thickness of the slices is important when frying meat, because too-thin slices will become leathery, and too-thick ones will not cook through evenly. Usually veal *girello* is about 2½ inches (6 to 7 cm) across; therefore you should estimate 2 slices for each person. Cut the membrane around the slices here and there with a sharp knife, to prevent the cutlets from curling while they're frying.

Beat the egg with a pinch of salt. Dip each veal slice into the egg, allowing the excess egg to drip off before you proceed with the breading. The bread crumbs should be dry, to prevent any lumps from forming during the operation. Put the bread crumbs in a tray and dredge each slice through them. When a first layer of crumbs has stuck to the meat, lay it on the crumb mound and press down. Repeat the dredging and pressing on both sides. As you finish them, lay the breaded slices onto a dry dish.

Over medium flame, heat enough oil to half-cover the veal cutlets in a large skillet. When the oil is hot enough, a single crumb of bread dropped in it should sizzle. Fry the cutlet, no more than 4 or 5 at a time—the better to monitor the cooking. When the cutlets have turned a nice deep golden color on the bottom, turn them and fry until both sides have the same color, about 2 minutes on each side. Transfer them to a piece of paper that can absorb the excess oil without sticking to the meat. Avoid stacking the slices; they will drain better in a single layer. Sprinkle each one sparingly with salt, cover with a tablespoon of the raw tomato sauce or a teaspoon of the anchovy sauce, and serve immediately.

RAW TOMATO SAUCE
Makes 1 cup (250 ml)

3 or 4 fresh, ripe plum tomatoes, seeded
2 cloves garlic, chopped
1 tablespoon minced flat-leaf parsley
2 tablespoons (30 ml) extra virgin olive oil
1 tablespoon (15 ml) red wine vinegar
Salt

This sauce needs a few fully ripe tomatoes, preferably plum tomatoes of the San Marzano variety. Cut the tomatoes into small cubes about ½ inch (1 cm) across. Put them in a mixing bowl with the garlic, parsley, oil, vinegar, and a pinch of salt. Leave the tomatoes to rest for a few minutes while you fry the veal. Estimate an abundant tablespoon of the tomato mixture to go with each veal cutlet.

ANCHOVY SAUCE
Makes ¾ cup (170 ml)

2 tablespoons (50 g) capers, drained
10 to 12 salted anchovies, boned and rinsed (see Choosing Ingredients and page 116)
2 tablespoons (30 ml) extra virgin olive oil
2 teaspoons (10 ml) red wine vinegar

Chop the capers finely on a board together with the anchovies. This is a moderately time-consuming operation, because the resulting mixture should be almost a paste, as smooth as you can get it. When it's the right consistency, put this paste in a bowl and blend it with the olive oil and vinegar, using a spoon. Do not add salt. This sauce has a very strong taste, so a teaspoon will be enough for each veal cutlet.

To me, cooking means to take control of the sensory changes in food brought about by combining and heating them. The principle of "whole, raw foods" cannot unconditionally apply to all edible things, because many types of food require long cooking; some types of meat and vegetables and a lot of other foods would be excluded from our diet if not adequately cooked. Therefore I reject the doctrine that equates cooking with "torture" or perversion of food's true nature. Rather, my main objective is to help you find a balance between an ingredient's natural qualities and those that it takes on as a result of cooking, and as you combine it with other ingredients to produce new flavors and tastes. Sometimes the quality of a raw ingredient will give a little hint of what it will add to a combination when it is cooked with other ingredients.

Parmigiana di melanzane

EGGPLANT PARMESAN

Serves 6

2 pounds (1 kg) very ripe fresh or canned tomatoes, peeled and finely chopped

3 or 4 cloves garlic, thinly sliced

4 pounds (2 kg) long, thin eggplants (aubergines)

2 cups (500 ml) extra virgin olive oil

Salt

1 bunch basil

10 ounces (280 g) fresh buffalo mozzarella, thinly sliced (see Choosing Ingredients)

7 ounces (200 g) provola affumicata (smoked provolone cheese), thinly sliced

1½ cups (185 g) grated Parmesan cheese, plus more for serving

♦

Parmigiana di melanzane

Eggplant Parmesan is one of the best dishes of Neapolitan cooking, which, in its turn, is one of the most interesting regional cuisines of Italy. This dish has become a standard in Tuscany and throughout Italy. People say that it is good even if badly prepared, and that it is almost impossible to make it badly. Many versions of this dish exist. The author of the one given here is Mrs. Passaro of Naples, who every Wednesday used to entrust (with an adequate tip) the conductor of the intercity Naples-Florence train with a neatly packaged baking dish containing *Parmigiana di melanzane* for her son, a reporter for a Florence newspaper who was homesick for Mother's cooking. Every Wednesday night, punctually at 7:00, he took delivery of the baking dish, ready for the oven, from the obliging railwayman. His friends often benefited from her demonstration of motherly love, and I can testify that her effort was worth it.

Because it is rather demanding in its preparation, the exact number of servings is never estimated—one makes a couple of casseroles of it to serve as a main course, and often it is all eaten at one time. But if there is some left over, so much the better; whoever feels like visiting the refrigerator will be very happy.

You will need eggplants of the narrow, long variety, fully ripe tomatoes, and three cheeses: *mozzarella di bufala*, a soft cheese made with buffalo milk; *provola affumicata*, a medium-hard, tangy, smoked cheese made of buffalo milk as well; and Parmesan. Unless the cheese department of your local market is very good, you may need to visit an Italian grocery store. You may cook the tomatoes, making a true *pomarola* sauce, but I prefer the version in which

the tomatoes cook in the oven together with the eggplant because the preparation looks fresher and avoids any taste of acidity.

In a bowl, combine the tomatoes and the garlic. Cut the eggplants crosswise in ½-inch- (1-cm-) thick slices. Do this with some accuracy, because in this instance thickness is important. Pour the oil in a skillet and heat over high heat. Very hot oil allows the slices to be crunchy gold outside without cooking too much inside. When the oil begins to smoke, start frying the slices 4 or 5 at a time, for about 4 to 5 minutes until golden. If the oil is deep enough to completely immerse the slices, you do not need to turn them; otherwise, turn them halfway through the frying time. Drain each slice well on absorbent paper, sprinkling salt on both sides; never stack the slices.

Fill two 9 by 13-inch (20 by 30-cm) baking dishes as follows: Place a few spoonfuls of tomato at the bottom, then add a single layer of eggplant slices. Cover them with more

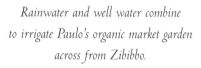

Rainwater and well water combine to irrigate Paulo's organic market garden across from Zibibbo.

tomato, then with basil leaves, and then mozzarella and provolone slices. Top with 3 to 4 tablespoons (20 to 30 g) of Parmesan cheese. Start again with an eggplant layer and repeat with the other ingredients. You should make at least 3 layers of eggplant and 2 of filling, finishing with an eggplant layer topped by tomatoes only. Bake uncovered at 325°F (160°C) for 30 to 40 minutes. Allow to cool before serving. It may be eaten lukewarm or even cold, but never straight from the oven. The dish needs no accompaniment, though you may add more grated Parmesan to serve.

Insalata de carciofi e parmigiano
ARTICHOKE AND PARMESAN SALAD WITH LEMON AND PEPPER DRESSING
Serves 6

6 artichokes
⅓ cup (75 ml) extra virgin olive oil
2 tablespoons (30 ml) freshly squeezed lemon juice
Salt
Freshly ground black pepper
1 cup (125 g) shaved Parmesan cheese

I recommend you use this dish as a second course, to finish the meal, because raw artichokes have a slightly bitter taste that lingers in the mouth and does not combine well with wine or other foods. Choose artichokes that are tender and fresh enough to be eaten raw.

Remove all the tough external leaves and wash the artichokes thoroughly (see page 109). Cut the artichokes in half lengthwise. Lay the artichoke halves on a chopping board with the cut side down and slice them as thinly as you can, eliminating the stem, which may be too bitter. Put the slices in a bowl and dress them immediately with the oil, lemon juice, salt, and pepper to keep them from discoloring. Place the slices on individual plates and cover with small, thin shavings of Parmesan cheese. Use *small* shavings: Very often, especially in restaurants where this simple dish is served, you find slices of Parmesan that are thin but the size of a bedsheet. These may look good, but they are not so good for the taste. Too big a piece of such a tangy cheese envelops the whole mouth, and you can kiss any other flavors good-bye.

Funghi trifolati
Fresh Porcini Mushrooms with *Nipitella*
Serves 4

4 fresh porcini mushrooms (see Choosing Ingredients)
3 tablespoons (50 ml) extra virgin olive oil
1 small bunch nipitella (wild catmint), leaves only (see Choosing Ingredients)
1 clove garlic, slivered
1 fresh or canned tomato, peeled
Salt
Freshly ground black pepper
Pinch of chopped fresh chile pepper (see Choosing Ingredients)

This final dish is a great one, but it is not exactly cheap, since it requires fresh porcini (*Boletus edulis*), a top-quality mushroom not easy to find fresh outside the Mediterranean region. The truly indispensable ingredient for this recipe is *nipitella*, a fresh wild herb of the mint family. In Tuscany, fresh *nipitella* is usually given away with the porcini, but it is not readily available everywhere and it is not replaceable. Fresh porcini mushrooms can sometimes be found at high-quality food stores.

I know of two versions of this dish, whose difference lies not so much in the recipe, but in the purpose. If you have several guests for dinner, you may use both the caps and stems (the latter must be thoroughly cleaned, and a longer cooking time will be required). If you have one mushroom for each guest, I suggest you enjoy the caps only, cooked just a few minutes. The stems can be left to dry (in a shady place), and eventually be cooked with *carnaroli* rice to make a good risotto. I prefer the latter variation.

Try this dish if you can find the ingredients. The execution is very quick, no more than 10 minutes for both preparation and cooking. Serve it as a side dish with roasted meats, such as lamb or pork.

Clean the caps with care, using a wet cloth or just a trickle of water, if necessary; they must not get too wet. Slice the caps ½ inch (1 cm) thick. In a nonstick pan with a cover that fits it well, put the oil, *nipitella* leaves, garlic, tomato, salt, black pepper, and chile pepper. Cook over high heat for 1 to 2 minutes. When the oil begins to sizzle, add the sliced mushrooms, turn the burner off, and cover the pan as tightly as possible. Leave it to rest for a few minutes, then serve hot.

Nipitella (above)
and fresh porcini mushrooms (right)

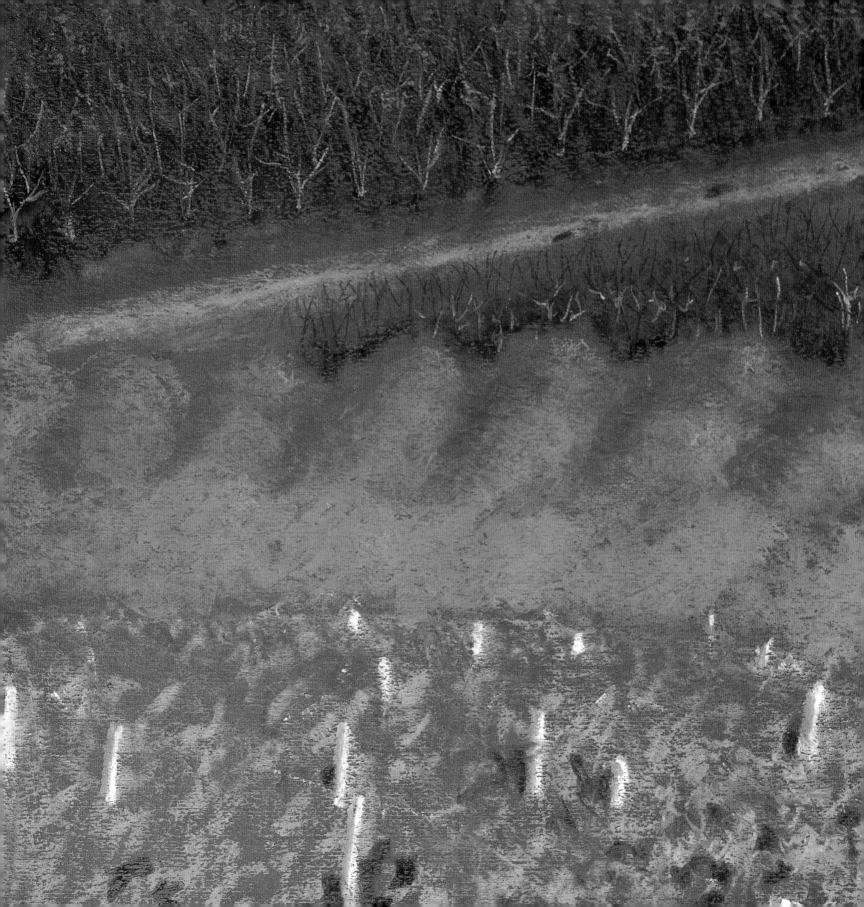

Bread, Oil, and Wine

bread, oil, and wine

Olive groves and vineyards make up the pattern of the land in Tuscany, covering most of the land that is not forested. Often the grapevines and olive trees grow in the same fields in alternate rows. We have an age-old tradition of olive cultivation and olive oil production.

Usually produced by blending at least two varieties of olives, Tuscan olive oil is among the most valued in Italy. The trees are treated with the utmost care. The olives are picked by hand, one by one, to enable the fruit to remain unbruised and fresh up to the moment of cold pressing. It is indeed heavy work. Considering that it requires so much care to produce the very best olive oil, its high price on the retail market is understandable. It is as precious a product now as at any time in the past.

The same applies to wine. Until not long ago, there was a period of mass production of poor-quality Chianti, mostly for export worldwide, trading on its prestigious name. In the last twenty years or so, though, the trend toward producing enormous quantities of shabby wine has been replaced by a commitment to the quality of the product, restoring the wine to the standards and reputation it deserves.

◆

A winemaker at Fattoria Castelvecchio checks the color of grape juice during the fermentation process. (above)

◆

November in Tuscany means olives ripe for the picking. (left)

I will not be so parochial as to claim that our region has any great superiority over others, but it is a fact that Tuscany has unusual wine-producing characteristics, due to its geographic location, its soil, its climate, and the imprint of centuries of human ingenuity. I believe that these characteristics should be upheld, protected, and treasured as a source of wealth.

Another important element of Tuscan culture is bread. It is nowadays more and more difficult to buy really good bread, although for centuries it has been the staple food of the region. Tuscan bread is born *sciocco*—"simpleton" in Italian, but in the local jargon it just means "without salt"—befitting its function as a neutral companion to any tasty food.

In the past, a loaf of bread often accompanied little more than itself on the dinner table, but that little was enough to make a meal.

No fat whatsoever is added to our bread, which stays fresh for a week or more. This kind of "shelf life" was developed at a time when bread was made only once a week—when one could not just cross the street to the bakery. One whole day a week was devoted to bread making, and baking was done in a communal village oven. Tuscan loaves are rather big, and the external crust insulates the soft interior from the surrounding air, keeping it from drying out. The leavening agent is a small amount of the previous week's dough, set aside in a suitable place. In seven days, enough live yeast develops to raise the new dough to a compact loaf with many tiny air bubbles, which form an additional defense against staleness.

The topic of bread would not be complete without mentioning the *madia,* a large wooden box with a hinged lid. It was the essential piece of furniture in all peasants' kitchens. Bread was kneaded on it and kept in it, together with anything necessary for making the bread. It was an implement made and used for one purpose only, but a vital purpose indeed. Nowadays we may still find *madie,* restored and valued as antiques, perhaps placed next to microwave ovens in sophisticated kitchens. Today they are certainly not used to keep bread, let alone make it; shiny and spotless, towering over modern implements, they bear witness to long-ago culinary practices and a way of living. Some who use them to store the fine Richard-Ginori porcelain set, or the bright stainless steel kitchenware, do not even know about their original purpose. Once, tireless and skilled women's hands toiled over them, their only purpose to fill bellies, with neither constraints of diet nor food science knowledge, but only the need to satisfy a hunger of which today we do not have the faintest idea.

◆

Quoting from *The Aleph* by Jorge Luis Borges, "I have a feeling that my birth was somewhat later than my residence here. I was already a resident when I was born here." I feel embarrassed when I have to talk about the links between humans and the earth—it is so easy to fall into the commonplace. One can talk for hours on end, try detailed or even poetic descriptions, list all its artistic and natural beauties, and still miss the essential point of the emotional ties one has developed with the land. Perhaps I might express these ideas in the form of a letter to a hypothetical lover who is coming to meet me in Tuscany.

◆

Antonio and Premitta Calvelli prepare the dough for schiacciata. These flat loaves are used as timers and are placed in the wood-fired oven with traditional Tuscan bread. When they are fully baked, Antonio can judge how much longer to cook the other breads.

My dearest, you write that you're about to leave and soon you will come to join me. You cannot imagine my joy at the prospect of having you with me again. I am thinking of everything we'll do together; while writing I am selecting in my mind the places best suited to discover the wonders of this land, this land that people from all over the world come to visit.

Sure we'll visit museums and monuments, but in order to understand at least part of my feelings, I want you to catch the atmosphere of the streets. I want you to understand the mood of the alleys, narrow and damp, paved with disjointed stones, where still craftsmen work, where small stores and workshops are still open; where people in overalls talk loudly from one door to the next.

There are city corners I especially love, little places full of atmosphere and magic. I will, without a guidebook, let you smell these places. I want you to see them before they disappear altogether.

Be ready to walk a lot, I will only allow you to rest enough to see the shade of the palaces creeping over the paving stones of the square where we'll sit down at a small table, sipping coffee. I'll lead you to the same place we will have visited in full sunlight, at sunset, when everything becomes golden, only to fade out in the dim light of the street lamps. I'll compel you to eat a panino con il lampredotto—a boiled tripe sandwich—the greatest glory of Florentine street-eating. Ah! How much I wish the many places of my youth still endured, to introduce you to them; pity many of them will only exist in my memory. Stopping in front of a shop of fashion handbags I'll tell you, "Here wonderful tuna sandwiches were sold, a meeting point for all truants; here they made coccoli (fried dough); there the pistachio ice cream: Grandpa used to bring me here when I was a child."

◆

Flowers are placed on religious shrines
in the streets of Florence.

Then we'll go out in the country, where you'll find the same colors as in certain places of the city. No wonder—Tuscany has her own palette, the hues of its stone, brick, soil, and vegetation. Unsealed roads white with dust go up and down, following the undulation of the hills, leading to vineyards, olive groves, and houses where you'll find those special colors again.

Yes, you're right. You are thinking that there are not many places left where, looking around a full circle, you won't have to shut your eyes in some direction. It is indeed only too common to see a four-story apartment block with aluminum-framed windows under the walls of a medieval hamlet, but the walls are *still there to be seen, choosing the right viewpoint. Come on, don't start complaining even before arriving!*

Believe me, despite all, this land still offers astonishing beauties even to those who, like me, know her fully, and if sometimes man's foolishness and carelessness prompt an escape, she, sweet Tuscany, can still catch, ensnare, subdue, and enchant you.

Observe a diet for a few days, as you shall not escape the eating tour I will enforce upon you, but don't be wary: Our food is healthy and balanced, and has nourished the most excellent artists and writers. Nowadays it is called the Mediterranean diet, and is reputed to be the cure-all for that part of the world suffering from excess food.

I am longing to see you, happy to be your guide, and you may be assured that—with the exception of some inescapable venue—you'll not have a tourist's life.

Love, Benedetta

Now let me take you, my reader, on an imaginary eating tour of Tuscany, one in which we may indulge all our senses. We will seek every possible ingredient of pleasure without worrying about the cost (mental travels are among the cheapest).

In order to start our tour in a blaze of glory, our first stop will be in the poshest restaurant in the city—the most renowned, the one marked in the guidebooks with all possible stars, forks, cups, you name it.

Once seated at our duly booked table, under the lofty and self-assured look of the waiter, we may begin. Well, first, let's eliminate that waiter, who by now almost unnoticeably twists his mouth, judging your jacket not sufficiently fashionable. Next, let us eliminate the pictures on the wall (seldom noteworthy), the cut-glass goblets of extraordinary height, the silverware, the elaborate flower arrangements, the menu as large as a king-size bedsheet. Finally, if we manage to dispense with the very building, replacing it with the mottled shade of an oak grove, heated to the temperature of a cool, late May evening, we may say that the beginning is not too bad.

The table and chairs are still there, though. We may relax, leaning in our seats, and even put our elbows on the table, as His Haughtiness in the bow tie would not allow. On this table, where some leaves fall and midges land every now and then, somebody has laid salt and pepper, some bread, some oil, and some wine. It is true that we have given up formalities in exchange for relaxation, but we have not given up quality, so we shall have the best bread, oil, and wine available. At this moment, the friendly young waitress—who has replaced the waiter—begins to bring to the table the ingredients we need to finally start our meal.

The first thing she offers is a handful of peeled garlic cloves.

I do not give an English name for the following recipe and certain other dishes in this book because their Italian names connote specific, classic recipes, like minestrone or *ribollita*.

Fettunta
Serves 6

1 loaf Tuscan-style bread (see Choosing Ingredients)
2 to 3 cloves garlic, peeled
Salt
Freshly ground black pepper
Extra virgin olive oil, for serving

Having already introduced Tuscan bread, I need not reiterate that this is the bread to use, or at least something very similar. Cut into slices about ½ inch (1 cm) thick (better thinner than thicker) and toast in the oven, or if possible on a charcoal grill, in such a way that both sides are crunchy outside without drying out inside. Bring the slices to the table wrapped in a towel in order to keep them warm. Each person may dress them according to personal taste; rubbing a little garlic on one face of the slice, add a little salt and pepper, and drizzle on some oil, which will be properly absorbed by the bread if it has been correctly toasted. Serve *fettunta* as an appetizer.

◆

Fettunta con cavolo nero e cardi

Fettunta con cavolo nero e cardi
FETTUNTA WITH BLACK CABBAGE AND CARDOONS
Serves 6

Salt
2 pounds (1 kg) cardoons (see Choosing Ingredients)
8 to 10 leaves black cabbage (see Choosing Ingredients)
1 loaf Tuscan-style bread, sliced and toasted (see Choosing Ingredients)
1 to 2 cloves garlic, peeled
3 to 4 tablespoons (50 to 60 ml) extra virgin olive oil

I worry any time I give a recipe with black cabbage because this vegetable, of black-green color, used to be nearly impossible to find outside Tuscany. I recall dinners prepared in New York with black cabbage and Tuscan bread brought from home in suitcases! Nowadays, I am told that both of these can be found in better supermarkets. Anyway, if you come across this cabbage, strip the outer leaves away and use only the smaller and softer leaves. The peculiar character of black cabbage is its strong and almost bitter taste, so this dish has sharp flavor; therefore one should carefully select the right moment to serve it in the context of a meal. I don't suggest it as a side dish for delicate food, or even as an appetizer, as *fettunta* is usually served, but as a final course.

Clean, unthread, and cut the cardoons as described on page 186. In a pot over high heat, boil enough salted water to cover the cardoons. Turn the heat down to maintain a simmer and cook for about 20 minutes, until tender. Drain. In a separate pot, cook and drain the cabbage in the same way.

Rub the toasted bread slices with the garlic and cover them first with the cardoons and then the cabbage leaves. Drizzle the slices lavishly with the oil; usually you won't need to add salt, because the vegetables will have absorbed salt while cooking.

Fettunta con pomodori
FETTUNTA WITH TOMATO
Serves 6

2 fresh, very ripe tomatoes, seeded and cut into small pieces
Salt
1 teaspoon (5 ml) red wine vinegar
2 tablespoons (30 ml) extra virgin olive oil
6 to 8 leaves basil, torn into pieces
1 loaf Tuscan-style bread, sliced and toasted (see Choosing Ingredients)

In a bowl, mix together the tomatoes with a little salt, the vinegar, oil, and basil. Spoon a suitable amount of this mixture on top of each bread slice. It is best to prepare this dish on serving trays in the kitchen, and bring it to the table ready to eat. Don't worry if the tomato juice soaks into the bread a bit; it is okay as long as the bread is suitably toasted.

If our young waitress and the wine work their magic, we'll begin to feel we're in a state of grace, a harmony between our mood and Tuscany's sky. From now on we may dispense with a host, and simply enjoy the dishes that follow.

Panzanella
Serves 6

½ loaf stale Tuscan-style bread (see Choosing Ingredients)

1 clove garlic, minced

2 scallions (spring onions), white parts only, cut in thin strips lengthwise

6 to 8 ripe tomatoes, preferably fresh, seeded and cut into small pieces

1 cucumber, peeled and sliced

6 to 8 leaves basil, torn into small pieces

2 or 3 bunches green radicchio (optional)

1 cup (250 ml) extra virgin olive oil

3 tablespoons (50 ml) red wine vinegar

Salt

Freshly ground black pepper

As with most of the recipes in this chapter, *panzanella* represents the very essence of classic Tuscan cuisine. It is a dish that must be eaten in the heat of summer in order to be fully appreciated. It may be served either as an appetizer or as a first course.

Cut the bread into small pieces, place them in a bowl, and cover with water. Soak the slices for about 10 minutes, until they are very damp but not too soggy. In a serving bowl, combine the garlic, scallions, tomatoes, cucumber, basil, and radicchio. If the radicchio is very fresh and tender, you can use the whole leaf. Otherwise cut it into slices ½ inch (1 cm) thick. Take the bread out of the water and break it up by hand. Wrap it in a clean towel and squeeze out as much water as possible.

Just before serving, gently mix the bread, oil, vinegar, and some salt and pepper with the vegetables in the serving bowl. Taste and adjust the seasonings before serving. Because the bread will soak it up, dressing should applied liberally. The *panzanella* should be dressed just before serving, otherwise the salted tomato will lose water, which will soak the bread, giving the dish an unpleasant, almost mushy texture.

I have learned from long experience that *panzanella*, which may look like an extremely simple dish to prepare, is seldom made well. Certain tricks, such as properly squeezing the bread and balancing the ingredients and seasonings, are essential for preparing *panzanella* that is not—and I have tasted plenty that were—a disgusting bowl of mush tasting only of soaked bread.

VARIATION WITH TOASTED TUSCAN-STYLE BREAD

Here is a variation that enables us to overcome the difficulties and, I believe, to score a few points over the classic one, even when the traditional recipe is well prepared. The preparation of the vegetables is just the same; the change is in preparing the bread, which, in this case, is to be fresh. Cut it into slices about ¾ inch (½ cm) thick, trim off the crust, and slice into large cubes. Toast these cubes with the usual care, in order to make the outside crunchy without drying up the inside.

Toss the bread together with the vegetables in a serving bowl, dressing lavishly and turning many times to ensure that the bread absorbs both dressing and vegetable juice; serve as soon as possible.

Crostini con lardo
LARDO AND TOMATO SALAD SANDWICH
Serves 6

2 fresh, very ripe tomatoes, seeded and finely diced
Salt
½ teaspoon (3 ml) red wine vinegar
⅓ cup (75 ml) extra virgin olive oil
4 to 6 leaves basil, torn into small pieces
6 slices Tuscan-style bread (see Choosing Ingredients)
3 to 4 ounces (90 to 110 g) lardo, sliced very thin
  (see Choosing Ingredients)

Here is a good way to sample *lardo*, the traditional Tuscan salt pork. This makes a nice snack or a first course at lunch.

Carrara marble cutters enjoyed a lunch
of Tuscan bread, lardo, and wine
in the crisp mountain air
of Colonnata. *(left)*

♦

Traditional lardo di Colonnata
is still made in the same way as it was
during the Roman Empire. Pork fat slabs
are brined with salt, rosemary, nutmeg,
and other spices and preserved
in large Carrara marble boxes,
which are then stored in cool caves
for eighteen months. *(below)*

In a bowl, combine the tomatoes, a little salt, the vinegar, oil, and basil. Toast the bread so as to leave the inside soft and the outside crisp. Place the slices of lardo on the warm bread, add a tablespoon of the tomato salad to each, and serve.

◆

My love-bonds with the next two recipes are particularly strong, as these were the staple foods of the first years of my adult life. In Florence, there used to be a restaurant where these dishes were made in a sublime way, and our limited supply of money was devoted to eating there. These dishes, wolfed down with the hunger and good humor of the eighteen-year-old, conditioned the choices of my life, and are largely responsible for my initial decision to become a restaurateur.

Still, they are humble dishes, born of the need to never throw food away, a philosophy that is far from our present way of thinking. I hear a bewildered old man…"Four bags of stale bread, big like that," he gestures with a lifted hand. "They…my son-in-law and my daughter…they have thrown them away!" He is not so much distressed at the waste of money as he is indignant over the waste of a substance that, for him, still has an intrinsic value beyond its worth in money.

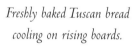

Freshly baked Tuscan bread cooling on rising boards.

Pappa al pomodoro

Serves 6

1 large red onion, minced

1 stalk celery, minced

1 carrot, peeled and minced

⅔ cup (150 ml) extra virgin olive oil, plus ½ cup (125 ml) for serving

2 pounds (1 kg) fresh or canned whole tomatoes, peeled

Salt

3 cloves garlic, finely chopped

1 loaf stale Tuscan-style bread (see Choosing Ingredients)

20 leaves basil, cut in small strips

This tomato bread soup was created in order to not waste old bread. Because of the very simplicity, one may say, poverty, of the ingredients, basil will stand out as the indispensable element of this soup. This dish should be made only in the summer, when basil is in season, and when it is also a pleasure to enjoy it at room temperature as a first course. Choose the most potently scented variety of basil you can find.

Start with a soffritto. Over medium heat, brown the onion, celery, and carrot in an aluminum stockpot with the ⅔ cup of oil. Sauté, stirring frequently and watching constantly. To ensure that the vegetables are soft enough, after about 5 to 7 minutes pour a ladle of water in the pot and, when it has all but evaporated, finish up the soffritto, stirring carefully until it is an intense golden color, about 15 minutes in all.

Now add the tomatoes, mash them with a fork, and add salt and garlic. (The amount of garlic may vary with taste, but a good tomato soup calls for quite a bit—say 3 cloves with our quantities.) Cook over medium heat for about 20 minutes, stirring occasionally.

While the tomatoes are cooking, break up the loaf of bread coarsely, and soak it in water for 10 minutes or so, until it is thoroughly wet, but not soggy. When it is soaked, break the bread into small pieces and then squeeze as much water out of them as you can in a clean towel. Toss the bread into the tomatoes after they have been cooking for about 20 minutes and stir well with a whisk to allow the bread to soak up the tomatoes. Cook the soup for another 5 minutes and then remove it from the stove. Stir in the basil. Also stir in the ½ cup of oil, for a smoother texture. Let the soup stand for a while, and never reheat it. Serve at room temperature, adding a dash of oil to each bowl.

Ribollita

Serves 6

1 red onion, minced

2 stalks celery, 1 minced and 1 finely chopped

3 carrots, peeled, 1 minced and 2 finely chopped

1 or 2 small prosciutto rinds (see Choosing Ingredients)

1⅓ cups (325 ml) extra virgin olive oil, plus more for serving

3 potatoes, peeled and finely chopped

2 zucchini (courgettes), finely chopped

¼ savoy cabbage, cut in ¼-inch (½-cm) strips

6 leaves black cabbage, finely chopped (see Choosing Ingredients)

4 leeks, white and tender green parts, sliced

2 cloves garlic, finely chopped

1½ cups (250 g) cooked white cannellini or navy beans, cooking liquid reserved (see page 106)

3 to 4 cups meat stock (see page 24)

1 small bunch wild thyme

Salt

1 loaf Tuscan-style bread (see Choosing Ingredients)

This is one of the best-known Tuscan bread soups. It is made of leftover ingredients. In Italy, the word *ribollita* ("boiled again") nowadays is considered rather disparaging. Years ago, the word indicated a continuous cycle of food utilization, where the leftovers were normal ingredients like anything else and not little, suspicious-looking bits of carrion forgotten in the refrigerator and waiting for the rubbish bin, as is usual today. It is served as a first course in the winter.

Start with the soffritto. Brown the onion and the minced celery, minced carrot, and prosciutto rinds in ⅓ cup (75 ml) of the oil over medium heat until it is medium brown, about 10 to 15 minutes. Add a little water if necessary to keep the soffritto from becoming too crisp. When the soffritto is done, toss in the potatoes, zucchini, chopped carrots and chopped celery, savoy cabbage, black cabbage, leeks, garlic, and the beans with all of their cooking liquid. Add meat stock as necessary to cover all the vegetables. Tie the thyme into a bouquet garni with a piece of string and add it to the soup. As the soup cooks, add salt to taste. Cook uncovered over low heat for about 30 minutes.

Meanwhile, break the bread coarsely in your hands and soak it in cold water for 10 minutes, until it is thoroughly wet but not soggy. Dry it by wrapping it in a clean towel and squeezing it well. The last vegetable to be done is the black cabbage, so when it is tender but still firm, take the pot off the stove and remove the thyme. Add the bread and the remaining oil, blending with a wooden spoon until smooth and creamy. Taste for salt.

Ribollita is usually prepared in advance, so leave it to rest for a few hours in order to enhance its taste. However, it is also a winter soup, to be served hot. When you are nearly ready to serve it, reheat gently over low heat, stirring continuously to prevent sticking. Serve hot with a dash of oil in each bowl.

With this method the result will be rather refined; that is, the *ribollita* will be creamy and smooth. I also appreciate a rougher version, obtained through another procedure, as follows.

Variation with Dry Bread

Prepare the ingredients and cook the vegetables exactly as above, but don't soak the bread. Ideally, the bread you use in this version should not be completely dry—rather old, yes, but still amenable to being sliced.

When the vegetables are cooked, take a large earthenware pot, pour some of the vegetable soup on the bottom, and lay slices of bread on the soup. Pour soup over the bread, and continue with alternating layers of bread slices and more soup. At the end, add as much meat stock as the bread absorbs. Cover the dish and let it stand until just before you are ready to serve. It is not necessary to refrigerate it during this period unless you have prepared it a whole day in advance. At the time of serving, stir well until evenly moist and gently reheat over a low flame, stirring continuously to avoid sticking or burning. Serve with a dash of oil as usual.

♦

Leeks in a garden

Many of the olive trees
growing on the hillsides above Antella
were planted in the eighteenth century.

The notes on the next three dishes (it's a bit of an exaggeration to call them recipes) are presented in this chapter only to indicate side dishes suited to the enjoyment of good olive oil, the extra virgin kind. Taste raw olive oils whenever you can so you learn to recognize good ones.

Spinaci scottati
BLANCHED BABY SPINACH
Serves 6

2 pounds (1 kg) baby spinach leaves, washed
Extra virgin olive oil, for serving

The spinach leaves must be really tiny, if possible without their stems, suitable for eating when they are just blanched. Put ½ inch (1 cm) of slightly salted water in a pot over high heat. When the water boils, toss in the spinach, cover, and let cook about 1 minute. Uncover, stir with a wooden spoon, and boil for another minute. Drain thoroughly, leaving the spinach in the colander about 10 minutes. If the spinach is still damp at the time of serving, gently press out the excess water with the back of a fork, taking care not to damage the leaves, which lose their flavor if treated so.

Serve the spinach in a communal bowl as a side dish with any main course. Each diner will dress it with oil on the plate, so the quality of the oil is paramount.

◆

An espresso cup is used to measure extra virgin olive oil.

Spinaci saltati
SAUTÉED SPINACH
Serves 6

2 pounds (1 kg) baby spinach leaves, washed
½ cup (125 ml) extra virgin olive oil
2 or 3 cloves garlic, sliced
1 fresh hot chile pepper, coarsely chopped (see Choosing Ingredients)
Salt

Blanch the spinach as in the above recipe. When it has drained, cut it gently into strips with a knife on a chopping board. Take care not to mince or mangle the cooked spinach, which will be quite fragile.

Heat the oil, garlic, and chile pepper in a pan over medium heat, stirring so the garlic doesn't burn as the oil heats. When the oil begins to sizzle, add the cut spinach and cook for about 5 minutes. Turn the spinach gently every now and then with a wooden spoon, so it will take in the other flavors. Taste, adjust for salt, and serve hot.

Insalata di finocchio
FLORENTINE FENNEL SALAD
Serves 6

3 or 4 white fennel bulbs
⅓ cup (75 ml) extra virgin olive oil
Juice of 1 lemon
Salt
Freshly ground black pepper

This fennel salad is a simple dish, originating in our custom of eating raw vegetables *in pinzimonio,* wherein each person at the table prepares his or her own dressing in a small bowl, and then dips pieces of any sort of vegetable, such as artichokes, fennel, celery, carrot, zucchini, and so on, into the dressing. The only rule for this way of eating is the choice of the extra virgin olive oil: It must be from the current year, cold pressed, and without acidity. Serve as an accompaniment to meat or fish dishes.

Choose fennel bulbs that are white and tender enough to be eaten raw. Trim and set aside the green stalks, which are tougher; they may be used later in a cooked dish. Wash the bulbs well. Cut them lengthwise in quarters and then into lengthwise strips about ¼ inch (½ cm) wide. Put the strips into a salad bowl, toss them with the oil, lemon juice, and some salt and pepper, and serve.

Fennel

Calamari inzimino
Serves 8

⅓ cup (75 ml) extra virgin olive oil

1 red onion, minced

1 carrot, peeled and minced

1 stalk celery, minced

½ pound (250 g) fresh or canned tomatoes, peeled

3 cloves garlic, finely chopped

Pinch of ground chile pepper (see Choosing Ingredients)

Salt

2 pounds (1 kg) squid, cleaned and cut in rings

1 pound (500 g) Swiss chard, stemmed

1 pound (500 g) spinach, stemmed

⅔ cup (150 ml) dry red wine

½ loaf Tuscan-style bread, for serving (see Choosing Ingredients)

This classic recipe of Florentine cooking is one of the few traditional seafood recipes of our inland city. It is very tasty and spicy and is usually eaten with a lot of bread, which appeases one's hunger more than the squid itself does. The etymology of the word *inzimino* isn't exactly clear, or at any rate there are various interpretations of it: that it derives from the Arab word *samin* (fat, fleshy), from the verb *samana* (to oil a dish), or from *ciminio* (cumin), from which we would presumably arrive at *zimino*, meaning "a spicy sauce." This dish is usually served as a second, or main course.

Prepare a soffritto by heating the oil in a large saucepan over medium-high heat. Add the onion, carrot, and celery and sauté, stirring often and watching constantly, until the vegetables are medium brown, about 10 to 15 minutes. Then add the tomatoes, half the garlic (the quantity of garlic given here is just a suggestion; it can be more or less, according to taste), and an abundant pinch of chile pepper. Mash the tomatoes into the soffritto with a fork, and add salt with a light hand, as usual when cooking seafood.

Cook for another 2 or 3 minutes, letting the tomatoes blend a little into the soffritto. Add the squid, chard, spinach, and wine, maintaining a medium heat, and when the chard and spinach have wilted a bit into the sauce, cover and cook for 5 minutes. Next turn the heat down to very low, remove the cover, and cook for about 40 minutes, stirring

◆

Freshly picked grapes for Chianti (above)

◆

The hillside villa of Fattoria Corzano and its vineyard below (left)

occasionally. If the cooking liquid is still too thin after this time, turn the heat up to high for a few minutes to reduce it to a creamy consistency. Remove from the heat and taste, adjusting the salt and chile if necessary (the *inzimino* must be piquant). Add the remaining garlic and leave the dish to rest for a while. Slice the bread about ½ inch (1 cm) thick and toast it in the oven, until it is crunchy outside and soft and warm inside. Reheat the *inzimino* over low heat before serving it on dinner plates with the bread on the side.

Stracotto al vino rosso
STRACOTTO WITH CHIANTI
Serves 8

1 small red onion, minced
1 carrot, peeled and minced
1 stalk celery, minced
⅓ cup (75 ml) extra virgin olive oil
2 pounds (1 kg) girello (veal top round), in one piece
1 teaspoon all-purpose (plain) flour
1½ cups (375 ml) Chianti or other red wine
⅓ cup (75 ml) meat stock (see page 24) or water
Salt

This is a main course, to be accompanied by spinach, green beans, or *Puré di patate* (see page 31).

Brown the onion, carrot, and celery in the oil in a large saucepan over medium heat just until the soffritto begins to take on a light golden color, about 5 to 10 minutes. Add the whole piece of meat and sauté together with the soffritto for 15 minutes, turning the meat gently to brown all sides. When both meat and vegetables are browned, mix in a teaspoon of flour, stirring continuously to avoid lumps. Pour in the wine and the stock and add a little salt. Turn down the heat under the pot and simmer, covered, for about 90 minutes. Turn the meat from time to time while cooking so that each part of it is submerged for a while in the liquid.

When the meat is tender to a fork, remove it from the pot, reserving the cooking juices. Slice it ¼ inch (½ cm) thick and serve piping hot, pouring abundant cooking juices over each slice.

Traditionally, students from Florence took a break from their academics to help with the grape harvest in the Chianti region. Now people come from all over the world to pick the grapes and taste the Tuscan way of life.

Cooking Techniques

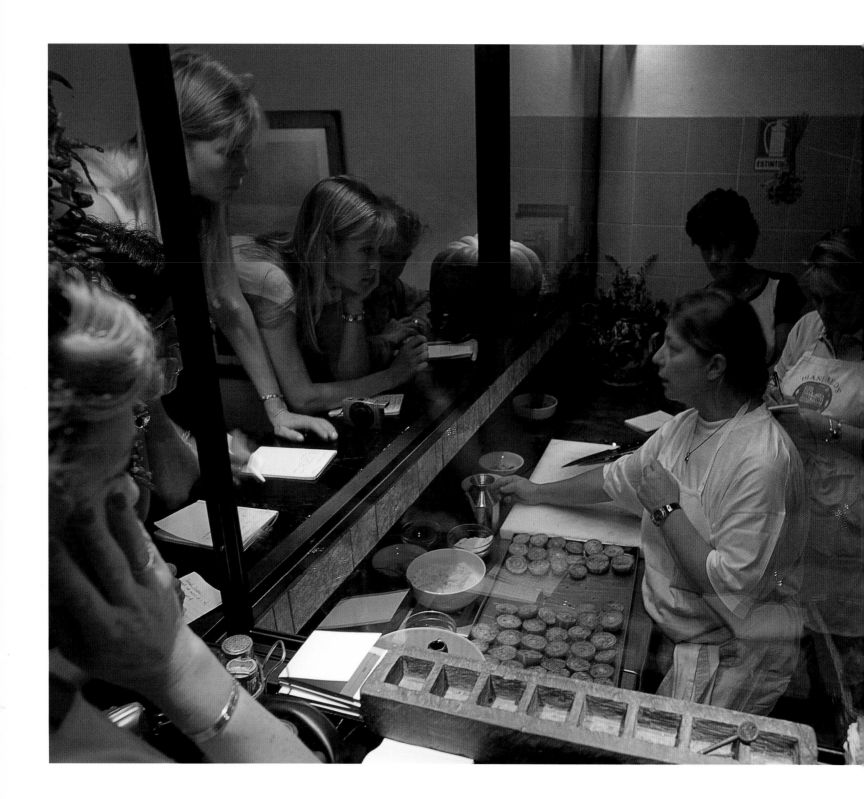

cooking techniques

This book is not intended for those who want hints on preparing formal banquets, but for those who are sick and tired of relegating their nourishment to frozen dinners and fast-food eateries and who crave a healthy, balanced, and enjoyable way of eating—for themselves and those they cook for. That is why I have chosen to include this chapter. The main purpose of the recipes here is to familiarize you with some of the common proce-dures you must know to cook in the Tuscan way. These techniques are simple in themselves, but they are manda-tory even for the least sophisticated cooking.

I want to encourage those who consider themselves hopeless as cooks: Just because you don't know any recipes, does not mean that you are unable to cook. There is always time to learn to make dishes for special occa-sions. Therefore, I dedicate this chapter to those who confess, "I don't know what to do with my hands." In particular, I dedicate this chapter to an attractive English girl I know who, following the directions on a package, carefully salted and boiled water, then tossed in a pound of spaghetti, including its plastic wrapping! If such a thing were done with the precooked stuff, the difference would hardly have been noticeable.

◆

Benedetta gives a cooking class to young Londoners. (left)

I am convinced that the major elements of food preparation are personal creativity, taste, and one's inclinations and habits. In the past, one developed such qualities only after gaining some expertise. Although cooks did not have formal training, they developed an understanding of common principles through simple observation, while performing everyday kitchen tasks. This common knowledge, enhanced by personal experience, evolved into the ability to cook.

Nowadays, this level of understanding is rare. Consider the family's use of the kitchen itself. Once it was the preferred meeting place of the people living in the house. Now it is merely a service room, often cramped and set apart. In the past, large kitchens were the cen-ters of our homes. Adults made coffee and schoolchildren did their homework or listened to their grandparents telling stories. We absorbed the acts of cooking without realizing it. Kitchens were busy places, and I think this was the reason why we liked to spend our time there. My family spent many moments of the day in the kitchen, in a sort of suspended time, consumed by neither work nor play—a way of living no longer common. Nowadays we are always busy, or we believe ourselves to be, even if we are just watching television.

I have a feeling of loss over those simple moments spent in the kitchen. When I think back on those times, my mind fills with pleasant reflections, sometimes disconnected, but woven together by the activities that form the tissue of life. "I have to cut the onion," my mother would say. "Move a little, or else you'll cry." So I would take my exercise book and go to the other side of the table. Before starting to write again, I'd look up at my mother, who was cheerfully weeping as she sliced the onion.

Skillet Cooking

Due to a shortage of time, the menu of everyday meals is often reduced to meat and salad. One quick method of cooking meat is on the griddle, which isn't always possible because few family stoves are equipped with them. Today they are usually replaced by wide, shallow skillets made of aluminum, cast iron, or tin-plated copper that transmit heat well. This first recipe contains several techniques that will help you learn to cook meat well using a skillet.

Filetto
FILLET OF BEEF
Serves 6

Extra virgin olive oil
6 (1-inch- or 2-cm-thick) boneless rib steaks or beef tenderloin (about 2 pounds or 1 kg total)
Salt
4 tablespoons (50 g) unsalted butter, for dressing (optional)
Juice of 1½ lemons, for dressing (optional)

Meat slices to be cooked in this way should not be too thin: Make sure they are at least ½ inch (1 cm) thick for boneless rib steaks, and 1 inch to 1½ inches (3 cm or so) thick for tenderloin. Any side dish can accompany this main course.

Lightly oil the meat slices on both sides, to prevent the surface from burning because of the high temperature. Meat cooked in this way must remain rare inside; any attempt to cook it until well done will make it hard and stringy. Because of this, the cooking should be carefully monitored.

Place a heavy-bottomed skillet over high heat. It is important that the skillet surface be very hot before you put the meat into it. This seals the fluids inside the meat, which otherwise will undergo a sort of boiling and become dry. To check the temperature, flick a drop of water into the skillet; if it sizzles, jumping all around, it is the right time to start cooking the meat. Steaks of the thickness suggested here should be cooked 3 minutes on each side, a bit less for thinner steaks and tenderloin.

Cook the meat first on one side and then the other. One detail that may help you decide when to turn the slices is this: When the heat has formed a crust on the meat's surface, the slice will come easily off the skillet or griddle. If you experience some resistance, cook it a little more. After lifting the slice off the skillet, wait a few seconds before putting it back down, allowing the surface to become hot again. Add salt only after cooking is complete.

The meat may be served as it is, or leave the skillet on the stove and put in the butter and a dash of oil, stirring briskly. Don't cook the butter, but when it is melted and hot, add some lemon juice (1 lemon for every 4 slices of meat), thus making a sauce to dress the meat just before serving.

Grilling

Grilling can be done in a fireplace, on a barbecue, or in the open over a campfire, if you know how to do it. Otherwise, use charcoal or learn how to select firewood. Not all woods are suitable because their aromatic smoke gives peculiar tastes to the meat. Softwood is to be avoided; oak is good and olive wood is even better.

Ideally, the steaks should be aged; however, meat aging is one of the butcher skills now all but disappeared—or in any case there is no commercial interest in stocking meat until it is aged enough. In Tuscany, the finest beef comes from grass-fed Chianina cattle. Chianina are now raised abroad in such beef-friendly countries as Argentina, the United States, Canada, and Australia, but it is not easy to find, even in Florence.

My family spent many moments of the day in the kitchen, in a sort of suspended time, consumed by neither work nor play — a way of living no longer common.

*Florentine steaks and spare ribs
ready for the grill.*

Bistecca alla fiorentina
FLORENTINE STEAK
Serves 6

1 (2-pound or 1-kg) T-bone steak, 1½ to 2 inches (3 to 5 cm) thick
Salt
Freshly ground black pepper

I must emphasize that if the quality of the meat isn't good, it is better not to cook in this way. First of all, I believe that a steak cannot be anything but rare. When I hear of people ordering a steak well-done, I feel sorry for them, because in this way not only does the meat become hard, but its taste is not what it should be. I think that those who like their meat well-done should choose other cooking methods, other recipes, or other food.

Start a fire in the grill, using plenty of wood or charcoal in order to obtain a good quantity of coals, which is important for cooking the meat properly. You can never have too many coals, because the more intense the heat, the shorter the cooking time, allowing you to obtain a nicely grilled outside without overcooking the inside. The embers should be about 6 inches (15 cm) below the grill.

Once you have put a steak on the grill, it must only be turned once, and the length of cooking depends on its thickness and on the amount of coals. Grill for 6 to 7 minutes on each side. Add salt and pepper only at the very end, and serve right off the grill, with any side dish.

Rosticciana
GRILLED SPARE RIBS
Serves 4

2 pounds (1 kg) pork spare ribs
Salt
Freshly ground black pepper
Juice of 2 lemons (optional)
2 or 3 cloves garlic, chopped (optional)

Spare ribs are pork ribs cut apart, a very tasty morsel that is also appreciated by children, who enjoy gnawing on the bones. Grilling is not the only way to cook them, but it's certainly one of the best because the ribs lose the excess fat and the outside of the meat becomes very crunchy.

Make your fire in the grill, using plenty of wood or charcoal in order to obtain a good quantity of coals. The embers should be about 6 inches (15 cm) below the grill.

The ribs may be cooked as they are, adding salt and pepper at the end. Or you may marinate them for a couple of hours before cooking in the lemon juice, pepper, and garlic. This makes them tastier, and the lemon juice gives them a fresh tang. Discard the garlic before cooking. Cook about 10 minutes on each side. When they are done, no trace of blood should remain near the bone. Serve piping hot with *Peperonata* (see page 124) or any other side dish

Oven Roasting

Oven roasting is a common method for cooking meats of various kinds. It is mistakenly considered very simple just because it is so ordinary, but I believe that it is not so simple if you expect excellent results. Properly roasted meat is soft and nicely cooked inside and evenly crunchy outside. A necessary element for obtaining a good roast is knowledge of how your particular oven works—that is, if the heat comes from the top or the bottom, and whether it is evenly radiated or concentrated in particular spots. If you know this, you can regulate your roasting as necessary. The best modern ovens overcome most of these difficulties, using forced air circulation (convection), humidifiers, and other gadgets aimed at making everything easier.

Anatra arrosto
ROASTED DUCK WITH RED WINE GRAVY
Serves 4 to 6

1 whole duck (4 to 6 pounds or 1½ to 2 kg), cleaned and plucked,
    neck and feet removed and reserved
1 cup (180 g) whole shelled chestnuts; 3 or 4 plums, pitted and cut in 2 to 4 pieces and
    2 apples, cored and cut in 4 pieces; or
    1 clove garlic, sliced; and 1 small bunch rosemary, for stuffing (optional)

Salt

⅓ cup (75 ml) extra virgin olive oil

1 red onion, coarsely chopped

1 carrot, peeled and coarsely chopped

1 stalk celery, coarsely chopped

2 teaspoons (10 ml) honey (optional)

Freshly ground black pepper (optional)

½ cup (125 ml) dry red wine

½ cup (125 ml) meat stock (see page 24)

This is a main course, and it's especially good with *Puré di patate* (see page 31).

Rinse the duck very well and dry it with a cloth. You can, if you like, stuff the duck with chestnuts, plums, apples, or with the clove of garlic and the rosemary. Salt the duck inside and out, rub it with the oil, and put it in a roasting pan. Add the onion, carrot, celery, and the neck and feet of the duck.

It's not easy to achieve a beautiful crisp skin when roasting so I will teach you a Chinese trick: In a small bowl, mix the honey with a little water, salt, and pepper, and baste the skin abundantly with this mixture before putting it in the oven. I promise you that it works.

Place the pan in the oven heated to 400°F (200°C), and after about 10 minutes, when the oil on the bottom of the pan starts to sizzle, add the wine and stock. Do not pour it on the duck, but rather in the bottom of the pan.

Roast the duck for 60 minutes (or more, if it's larger than specified). Check often to be sure that there is always some liquid in the pan; add more water if needed. Baste every 10 minutes with the pan juices. When the duck's skin is deeply golden and crispy take it out of the oven and let rest it 15 minutes before carving. Remove the wings and legs, slice the breast, and if the bird is large, slice the legs as well. Put the roasting pan on the stovetop over medium heat, and adjust the gravy, reducing it further if it is still too liquid, or stirring in a little stock if it is too thick. Remove the vegetables, neck, and feet and discard. Put the gravy through a strainer and serve it hot over the slices of duck.

◆

Fresh chestnuts litter
the hillside trails in October.

Arista

ROASTED PORK LOIN WITH GARLIC, LEMON ZEST, ROSEMARY, AND SAGE

Serves 8

4½ pounds (2¼ kg) pork loin roast, on the bone
2 cloves garlic, sliced
2 strips lemon zest, minced
2 to 3 teaspoons minced fresh rosemary
2 to 3 teaspoons minced fresh sage
Salt
Freshly ground black pepper
3 to 4 tablespoons (50 to 60 ml) extra virgin olive oil

♦

Arista

This method of cooking *arista* uses what remains of the techniques applied when an oven was a contrivance heated by burning wood inside and made of masonry, bricks, or even river stones, and was essentially used for baking bread. Almost every hamlet had one, used on a rotating basis by the village women, who paid a fee to cover the cost of the firewood.

An image surfaces in my memory of this custom, now well and truly disappeared. In Colfiorito, where my family used to spend the summer holidays, Sesta, a short, mustached peasant woman, had such an oven. The oven was in a small room adjacent to her house, where everything was blackened—walls, door, *madia*—but nothing was dirty, only sooty, just as she, the fire-keeper, was black but clean. She lighted the fire every day, sweating and handling various tools through the mouth of the oven, which was unevenly lit by the wobbling flames. Then she would turn toward us, gangs of urchins gazing with rapture at her operation, and smile with a toothless mouth.

Bread making was done in every house, begun the previous evening with the kneading of a mountainous heap of dough, which was left to rest overnight. The loaves were shaped in the morning, and put in rows wrapped into a long cloth. A rimmed plank about six feet (two meters) long and one loaf wide was loaded with loaves, covered, and balanced on the housewife's head on her way to the oven. I recall the way those women walked, the elegant and sober gait needed to keep their balance, their hands busy holding pots and pans. They moved silently and quickly among the urchins, who were made merry by the sense that something wonderful was happening.

When the bread was done, the *schiacciata* went into the oven. This was a sort of flat dough with oil, salt, and rosemary. It freed the women from the kids: "Go out and eat this!" At the end of all the baking, the oven temperature was much lower. This was the moment to put in those dishes requiring a whole night of slow cooking. In the morning, they would be perfectly cooked, and their owner would take them out of the oven just in time for Sesta to refill it with wood, beginning all over again the process of baking the bread, *schiacciata,* and cooking the roast of the person whose turn it was to use the oven that day. Sesta would begin toiling again, toothless, stooping, white with flour, and black as her oven.

This recipe utilizes the same slow-cooking technique that Sesta and those like her practiced many years ago. In addition to beans, which require very slow cooking, *arista* is prominent among the dishes to be cooked at very low heat. Cooked in this way, not only does it become very tender, but it keeps well for a few days and can be eaten cold, thinly sliced. It is, of course, a main dish. Accompany it with *Fagioli* (see page 106) or *Puré di patate* (see page 31). This roast is also very good cold with thin slices of raw onions, dressed with oil.

Carve the meat off the bone with a sharp knife, both on the rib and the fillet sides, keeping the meat in one piece. Pierce the meat on the rib side several times with a long, thin knife. Combine the garlic, lemon zest, rosemary, and sage in a bowl with abundant salt and pepper. Spread the mixture on the deboned side of the meat, and fill up the holes on the rib side, pushing the mixture inside with the handle of a wooden spoon.

Reassemble the meat onto its bone as it was beforehand, tying it together with some kitchen string. Lay it in a large aluminum roasting pan, sprinkling some salt on top and on the sides. Grandma used to say that roast meat could never be too salty, and I, despite not wanting to be considered an instigator of wrongdoing, reckon that what my grandmother said had a core of truth: Roast meat should be rather salty.

Pour a small amount of oil into the pan, just enough to make a protective film on the bottom.

Heat your oven to 225°F (100°C) if it's a regular oven, or 200°F (90°C) if you have a convection oven. Put the roast in the oven and let it cook for 4 hours. Check for doneness by piercing the meat with a sharp knife; it will be ready when no trace of blood gushes from the cut. *Arista* may be eaten as soon as it is out of the oven or served lukewarm after a rest.

Boiling

Nowadays, boiling is often replaced by other cooking methods that give better results and are more in keeping with retaining the wholeness of the food. As a matter of fact, the very immersion of food in water may dissolve its important nutrients and make the taste blander. Nevertheless, boiling is sometimes necessary, and it is useful to know how to eliminate the drawbacks of this method.

Branzino
POACHED SEA BASS
Serves 6

1 whole sea bass, about 2 pounds (1 kg)
½ red onion, cut in large pieces
1 stalk celery, cut in large pieces
1 carrot, peeled and cut in large pieces
2 tablespoons coarsely chopped flat-leaf parsley
2 tablespoons coarsely chopped fresh basil
Salt
Extra virgin olive oil, for serving
2 lemons, sliced, for serving

To have a properly poached sea bass, you need a fish poacher, which is an elongated pan equipped with a removable double bottom, into the top of which the fish is laid. Once the fish is cooked, the poacher allows you to lift it out of the water without breaking it. Serve this dish as a main course. Boiled potatoes are a good accompaniment.

Put a few inches of water in the bottom of the poacher and add the onion, celery, carrot, parsley, and basil. Salt the water very sparingly; fish should never be salted much or it may lose its specific taste. Place the fish in the top part of the poacher and lower it into the water, which should just cover it. Cover the poacher and put it over medium heat until the water starts boiling. Remove the pan from the fire right away and set it aside for 10 to 15 minutes, until the flesh is fully white and tender. Serve with oil and lemon on the table.

Aragosta o astice bollito

LOBSTER

Serves 6

6 North Atlantic or spiny lobsters,
1¼ to 1½ pounds (600 to 700 g) each
Extra virgin olive oil and 2 or 3 lemons, or
1 cup (250 ml) Mayonnaise (see page 166), for dressing

◆

Crayfish are commonly caught
in the large bilancia (balance) fishing nets
that are used on the canals
of Lake Massaciúccoli.

Cooking a lobster, a crayfish, or the like, is a difficult task that understandably many cannot do. The fact is that these crustaceans must be put alive into boiling water, and just thinking of it makes some people feel like persecutors of sea animals. I cannot blame them, and I would suggest, if they really like lobster, that they visit a good restaurant.

If you are not so concerned about the unfortunate end of these armored brutes, or if their wonderful taste is stronger than your pity, set about cooking them by preparing a large stockpot full of water. Place it over high heat, and when the water starts boiling, quickly plunge in the lobsters and cover the pot immediately. Spiny lobster should not cook for a long time, just 5 to 7 minutes per pound. North Atlantic lobster is usually cooked about 10 minutes per pound. Take them out of the water and serve them with oil and lemon, or with fresh mayonnaise, although I personally don't fancy the addition of sauces to seafood.

Of the many good ways to serve lobster, I prefer the simplest method. Cut lengthwise down the carapace from the head to the tail to make it easier for your guests to open the lobsters themselves. Provide the diners with whatever assortment of lobster crackers, nutcrackers, seafood picks, or shears you have, along with plenty of napkins, and let them dress the lobster themselves.

◆

In all kitchens, all over the world, one may find something similar to our *bollito*, that is, various types of boiled meat and vegetables. In Tuscany, we have many different ways to prepare boiled meat, depending on what is available and the circumstances. It can be a rich dish or a very meager one consisting of as little as bones, a few grams of meat, and seasonings, for low-calorie diets or for those who may be lacking protein or money.

A nice tray of varied boiled vegetables is a great dish, not to be underestimated, as it can be served at formal and informal dinners alike. Dishes of this sort are a little tiresome to prepare, especially because cleaning vegetables is one of the most time-consuming kitchen tasks. Take advantage of such a time to meditate, if you are alone, or, if someone is present, take the opportunity for a good chat.

In the first chapter I gave the recipe for boiled meat and meat stock, as made in Tuscany, which cannot be classified as a light food. It requires long cooking and as such is an endangered dish. It is indeed one of that large number of recipes to be handled with special care, as wildlife lovers do with their own endangered species. Now, here are some ways we boil vegetables to be used as side dishes with main courses.

Cavolfiore
BOILED CAULIFLOWER
Serves 4 to 6

1 head cauliflower
Extra virgin olive oil, for serving
1 lemon, cut in wedges, for serving

For most members of the cabbage family, boiling can be either the only method used to make them edible, or just a first step in the preparation. A good rule is to use as little water as possible, in order to prevent loss of taste.

Remove and discard the external, leathery leaves of the cauliflower, and wash the head well. Put it into a pot with just enough salted water to cover the stalk, which is the toughest part. The remainder will be cooked by the steam. Place the pot over medium heat and cover it tightly. After 10 minutes or so, check for doneness by piercing the stalk with a fork, taking into account two things: First, because of its compactness, cauliflower keeps heat inside for quite a while, and therefore will keep cooking for a few minutes even after it is taken out of the pot. Second, the cauliflower will be tastier if not overcooked, so the stem should be soft but still firm when tested with a fork. Separate the large branches of cauliflower by cutting them where they join at the stem and serve with a sprinkling of oil and lemon.

Fagioli
WHITE BEANS WITH PROSCIUTTO, TOMATO, AND SAGE
Serves 8

1 pound (500 g) white cannellini or navy beans (about 4 cups fresh or 2 cups dried)
3 or 4 cloves garlic, peeled
6 or 8 leaves sage
1 fresh or canned tomato, peeled (optional)
1 prosciutto rind, about 1 by 3 inches (2 by 7 cm), (see Choosing Ingredients) (optional)
Salt
Extra virgin olive oil, for serving
Freshly ground black pepper, for serving

Tuscans indulge in praising everything that has to do with themselves, and therefore they do not even suspect that there exists a huge variety of beans besides their own cannellini, considered the beans par excellence, and as such simply called *fagioli* (beans).

If you are using dried beans, soak them overnight in water to cover by 2 to 3 inches (5 to 8 cm). Drain, and in a stockpot, cover the beans with 2 inches (5 cm) of water. Add the garlic, sage, tomato, and prosciutto rind. Bring to a boil then turn the heat down to very low and cover the pot.

Beans require special attention. The best way is to cook them in a special earthenware pot, locally called a *fagiolaia*, which is large enough to contain all the required water. The earthenware prevents sudden changes in temperature. If you're using a metal pot, the flame should be kept very low in order to maintain a slow, not bubbling simmer.

For the same reason, beans should be stirred as little as possible, and never with spoons or other tools made of metal, which tend to cool the water. Just make sure that the beans simmer slowly and leave them alone; don't take the lid off. Usually, if they are

Braids of garlic hang
against the faded blue wall
of an old barn near Pomino.

On a sunny day,
large zucchini are left to dry
on top of an old pot.
They will produce seeds
for next year's crop.

fresh, 40 to 50 minutes will suffice; dried and soaked beans may require 10 to 20 minutes more. Taste the beans using a wooden spoon. When they are perfectly done, both the skin and the inner part will be soft. At this point, take the pot off the heat, throw in a handful of salt and gently stir; the beans will take their salt from the water.

Beans can be eaten as a side dish either hot or cold. Each person can dress them on the plate with oil and pepper, and a little more salt if needed.

Zucchine
BOILED ZUCCHINI
Serves 6

6 small zucchini (courgettes), ends trimmed
Extra virgin olive oil, for serving
1 lemon, for serving

To be sincere, *zucchine* (small zucchini or courgettes) are not the tastiest of vegetables. The "yuck!" of my children resounds in my ears when, performing the motherly task of preserving health, I serve a steaming tray of boiled zucchini. Nevertheless, many people like small garden zucchini, as fresh as possible, as they contain vitamins and have diuretic properties.

To cook them, toss them in boiling salty water, as little as needed to barely cover them, for about 10 minutes. Dress with the oil and lemon and serve with any main course.

Carciofi
BOILED ARTICHOKES
Serves 6

10 or 12 small artichokes
½ lemon, plus 1½ lemons cut in wedges, for serving
Extra virgin olive oil, for serving

Serve this as a side dish with any main course, especially lamb. Remove all the external, very hard leaves of the artichokes, and using a vegetable peeler or sharp paring

Nobody ever died from eating a sugar doughnut bought at a stall. Nevertheless, it is good to know what we are eating and to be attuned to the best of our attitudes, needs, and traditions.

knife, peel the bottom, stalk included, revealing the tender, pale green inner parts. Practice will help you judge how much of the artichoke must be discarded without excessive waste and without retaining leaves that will never cook. While you are learning it is better to be a little wasteful, to avoid serving leaves that are too hard to be chewed. Cut the cleaned artichokes lengthwise in quarters. If they are tender enough, you do not need to remove the choke; otherwise scrape it out of the quartered pieces. Put them in water into which half a lemon has been squeezed; otherwise they will blacken. Rub the same lemon over your hands if they are blackened by cleaning the artichokes.

Put a stockpot of salted water over high heat and bring to a boil. Put the artichoke quarters in the boiling water and cook uncovered for 10 to 15 minutes. When they are almost done, probe the bottoms with a fork for tenderness and taste a leaf or two. Drain when they are al dente—soft, but still crunchy. Serve hot, with the oil and lemon wedges.

Frying

Consider for a moment the most demonized of dishes: fried foods, cooked in deep, hot oil. Of course, eating fried food too often may be injurious to health, but if we respect the rules of moderation and sensible preparation, we may consider such food perfectly edible, and need not feel too guilty if we indulge in it from time to time. Nobody ever died from eating a sugar doughnut bought at a stall. Nevertheless, it is good to know what we are eating and to be attuned to the best of our attitudes, needs, and traditions as well.

Scientific research has determined that the chief hazard in this method of cooking lies in the toxic substances formed when oil reaches high temperatures for lengthy periods. Hence, we may devise methods that can minimize the adverse effects.

One of the most important elements is the choice of the frying oil. I suggest you use extra virgin olive oil whenever possible, because it is less likely to produce toxic substances than other oils. Alternatively, we may use soybean oil, which, being practically tasteless, does not influence the taste of the food. Other options are corn (maize) and sunflower oils, which may, however, unpleasantly interfere with the taste. I utterly discourage the use of cottonseed, canola (rapeseed), and unnamed vegetable oils and hydrogenated fats. Absolutely avoid margarine.

Butter deserves a special discussion, because butter-fried foods give excellent results in taste but are calorie-rich and hard to digest. I also strongly recommend against the use of deep-frying devices, because these entail an enormous waste of oil. It is indeed essential to throw away any oil already used for frying, never using it more than once; I am unconvinced of the usefulness of the purifying filters with which various contrivances are equipped. The classic frying pan may be used with modest quantities of oil, just as much as necessary, without prompting mourning when it is time to discard the oil.

Now, here are a couple of general suggestions that are likely to be useful. When frying for any length of time, skim off the scum from the oil every now and then with a skimmer, thus leaving the oil as clear as possible. Change the oil whenever you change the foods you are frying and after every three or four batches of breaded foods in a row. When you change the oil during a frying session, pour it very carefully into a metal container. The solid residue will settle on the bottom. Thoroughly clean the pan, using some paper to scrape away any residue. Pour the oil from the container (minus the specks from the bottom) into the pan again, topping it off with some fresh oil. Heat the oil to the proper temperature, and begin frying again.

A paramount variable in frying different foods is the oil temperature, which has to be very high at the moment you put in what you are frying, but then should be regulated depending on the food. When extra virgin

olive oil becomes very hot, it starts to form little bubbles and it becomes clearer. If it is too hot, it gives off an unpleasant burnt smell, and turns white and opaque. If this happens, discard the oil and start again. Using special frying thermometers, it is possible to exactly regulate the optimal temperature for frying each food, however, I won't expect such a level of technicality. Use whatever amount of heat is necessary to hold the oil at the prescribed temperature.

Almost all foods to be fried require some kind of preparation, and the operation may require the use of battering, flouring, or bread-crumbing. The preparation may be quite different for various types of food.

Maize hung to dry on a roof beam of an old barn near Pomino.

Pino Demurtas tends the flock at Fattoria Corzano & Paterno.

Cotolette d'agnello
FRIED LAMB CHOPS
Serves 6

1 egg
Salt
6 (½-inch- or 1-cm-thick) lamb loin chops
  (about 2 pounds or 1 kg total)
2 cups (200 g) dried bread crumbs
Extra virgin olive oil, for frying

Fried artichokes are a good accompaniment to this main dish.

In a wide shallow dish, beat the egg with a little salt. Put all of the lamb chops at once into the dish, coating them with egg on all sides. Withdraw the chops one by one by the protruding bone, drip off the excess egg, and lay each one onto a small heap of bread crumbs. Still holding the chop with your fingers, turn it over to coat the other side with bread crumbs. Then lay the chop on the crumbs and push it down with the palm of your other hand. Use one hand to hold the meat and the other hand to press it in order to avoid smearing the bread crumbs. Turn the chop over again and press its other side into the crumbs. As you finish them, lay the chops on a dry, flat surface near the stove, without overlapping.

Lamb should be well-done. Although the thickness of the chops (½ inch or 1 cm) may not require a long cooking time, it is mandatory for the heat to reach the bone; therefore slow frying is recommended.

Heat ¾ inch (1½ cm) of oil in your skillet over very high heat until little bubbles begin to form. Check the temperature of the oil by tossing in some bread crumbs; it is ready when they sizzle. Immerse the chops in the oil; don't overlap them. You may need to fry them in batches. In contact with the cold meat, the oil temperature will decrease, so wait for it to start to bubble again and then turn the flame to medium. Fry the chops for about 2 minutes on each side after the heat change and remove them from the oil when the crumbs have reached a deep golden color. Place them on absorbent paper to drain and sprinkle them with salt on both sides. Serve hot.

♦

Sheep raised at Fattoria Corzano &
Paterno supply the milk for making
its prized pecorino cheese.

Crocchette

BEEF AND POTATO CROQUETTES

Serves 6

1¼ pounds (575 g) boiling potatoes
1 pound (500 g) boiled beef (see page 24)
2 eggs
1 cup (125 g) grated Parmesan cheese
⅕ whole nutmeg, grated
Salt
Freshly ground black pepper
⅔ cup (90 g) all-purpose (plain) flour
Extra virgin olive oil, for frying

As with many other dishes, I daresay that croquettes, or *rissoles,* as they are also called, are made according to recipes to which every family claims the original patent. This recipe, however, is fairly widespread in Florence, and, in keeping with tradition, it is a recycled dish. A radicchio salad is a nice accompaniment to this main course. The weight of the potatoes should be a little more than that of the meat you have available.

Boil the potatoes in abundant water over medium-high heat, until they are cooked but still firm. When they are cool enough to handle, peel and put them through a food mill into a large mixing bowl. Mince the meat as finely as possible with a *mezzaluna* or a very sharp knife and, using your hands, mix it with the potatoes. Add the eggs, noting this caveat: Eggs are the cement of mixtures, and one has to be careful with the quantities because too little egg will not keep the ingredients together and too much will stiffen the whole thing. Two eggs should do nicely for these quantities.

Add the Parmesan, nutmeg, and some salt and pepper, taking care with the salt because the meat will already be salted from its boiling. Mix it very well with your hands. Now is the moment to shape and flour the croquettes. Put the flour in a wide, shallow dish. Wet your hands and form small handfuls of the meat and potato mixture into cylinders with rounded ends, a little over 2 inches (4 to 6 cm) long and about 1 inch (2 to 3 cm) in diameter. After you shape each croquette, roll it in the flour without pushing it out of shape. The flouring procedure is not that easy, because the croquette mixture is sticky, and even if it has been previously kneaded thoroughly, it may need to be worked a little more between the palms to keep it together.

Keeping your hands clean and wet can help. As you finish them, lay the croquettes on a dry, flat surface near the stove, keeping them from touching one another.

Pour enough oil in a frying pan, estimating an amount that will half cover the croquettes. Heat over a medium-high flame until rolling bubbles begin to form. It is important that the oil be hot enough because otherwise the croquettes will absorb too much of it. Croquettes don't need a long frying time because the ingredients are cooked already. However, you do want a nice even crust outside, so a strong flame should be used to fry them fairly quickly.

Drop the croquettes in the oil, making sure they don't overlap (you may need to cook them in batches). The oil temperature will go down when you first put them in, so raise the heat for 1 to 2 minutes to bring the temperature back up. Fry the croquettes for 4 to 5 minutes, turning them frequently, until they have a crispy golden crust. Croquettes tend to break up when turned. To avoid this, grasp them lightly between two spoons or forks and turn them with a single, quick motion. When they are done, quickly but gently remove them from the oil with tongs or a slotted spoon and lay them on absorbent paper. Sprinkle with a little salt, and serve very hot.

Calamari fritti
FRIED CALAMARI
Serves 6

2 eggs
2 tablespoons all-purpose (plain) flour
Salt
1 tablespoon (15 ml) milk (optional)
Extra virgin olive oil, for frying
1 pound (500 g) squid, cleaned and cut into rings about ½ inch (1 cm) thick

Batter is generally used for squid, but it can also be first floured and then dipped in egg, as in the *Acciughe fritte* (see page 116). Serve fried squid as a main course with a tomato and basil salad.

First, make the batter: Beat the eggs with the flour and a pinch of salt, and add a little milk if the egg and flour mixture comes out too thick for dipping. Pour enough oil in a frying pan, estimating an amount that will just cover the squid, and heat over a medium-high flame until little bubbles begin to form. Dip the squid rings into the batter and submerge them in the oil, taking care to keep them away from one another. Turn them at least once, and remove them with a slotted spoon when they're golden in color and crunchy on the outside; this should take 2 to 3 minutes. Squid may explode while cooking, causing nasty burns. To protect yourself, cover the pan with a wire gauze screen of the same diameter as the pan while frying, and be careful when turning the rings and when taking them out. Lay them on absorbent paper to drain briefly, and serve hot.

Acciughe fritte
FRIED ANCHOVIES
Serves 6

1 or 2 eggs
2 tablespoons all-purpose (plain) flour
Salt
1 tablespoon (15 ml) milk (optional)
1 pound (500 g) fresh anchovies, cleaned and boned
Extra virgin olive oil, for frying

"To hell with caviar and champagne, give me anchovies and white wine!" a fisherman I know from the Island of Elba used to say. He probably had tasted neither caviar nor champagne in his life, but he was immovable in his absolute certainty that nothing could be compared with anchovies. I would not be quite so radical, but I certainly agree with his appreciation of anchovies.

For this dish, you must have fresh anchovies. The drawback to fresh anchovies lies in their cleaning and boning, which needs to be done to ensure the happiness of everyone who will eat them. The operation consists of cutting open the belly and tearing away the head and backbone, trying to keep the fish in one piece and leaving the dorsal side intact. This is certainly a boring task, but not a difficult one, after one has some experience. Serve this dish as a main course with tomato or radicchio salad, or raw vegetables.

You may either coat the anchovies in a light batter, or, for crunchier anchovies, simply dust them with flour. If you choose to make a batter, which gives you a larger volume and a better look, beat 2 eggs with the flour and a pinch of salt. Add a little milk if it comes out too thick for dipping. Dip the anchovies into the batter right before frying. Or dredge the anchovies in the flour and then dip them into 1 beaten egg right before frying.

Pour enough oil in a frying pan, estimating an amount that will just cover the anchovies and heat over a medium-high flame until little bubbles begin to form. Put the anchovies in the oil, making sure not to overlap them. Fry for 2 to 3 minutes. The oil must be very hot, and should remain hot while frying, as anchovies do not require lengthy cooking. There should be enough oil in the pan to cover the anchovies so that you will not need to turn them while frying. Remove them from the pan with a slotted spoon and lay them on absorbent paper to drain briefly. Sprinkle them with salt before serving, more if they're floured, less if you have used a salted batter.

Mozzarella in carrozza
MOZZARELLA IN A BUGGY
Serves 6

8 ounces (250 g) fresh buffalo mozzarella, drained (see Choosing Ingredients)

2 ounces (50 g) salted anchovies

12 (½-inch- or 1-cm-thick) slices dry bread

6 leaves sage, chopped

1 tablespoon all-purpose (plain) flour

2 eggs

Salt

⅓ cup (75 ml) milk

Extra virgin olive oil, for frying

Mozzarella in carrozza is a typical Neapolitan dish. Since it is so difficult, I have included it here because once you have mastered it you will be ready to fry anything. Because of the difficulty of frying something that melts when exposed to heat, there is a remarkable wealth of methods aimed at solving such a problem. After trial and error, I believe the one detailed here to be the most suitable. The salted anchovies and sage are not included in the original recipe, but are additions I heartily suggest. A radicchio salad is a good accompaniment to this main dish.

Place the mozzarella in a dish, cover, and leave to drain overnight in the refrigerator so that it loses as much water as possible.

Cut the drained mozzarella into ½-inch (1-cm) slices. Rinse the anchovies thoroughly under a trickle of water. With your hands, open the back of each anchovy, remove the backbone, and divide into 2 fillets. Cut each of the fillets into 3 pieces. Now make "sandwiches" like this: a slice of bread, a slice of mozzarella, an anchovy fillet cut in 3 pieces, a chopped sage leaf, and a slice of bread. Holding together these sandwiches as well as possible, dredge their edges in the flour. Then beat the eggs thoroughly with a pinch of salt and the milk, trying to make this rather fluid batter as smooth as possible. Dip the "sandwiches" in the batter, first on one side and then on the other. The bread will soak up the liquid and become very floppy, hence the difficulty of frying it.

Put just enough oil in the skillet to submerge the lower bread slice and not quite reach the mozzarella (a little less than ½ inch or 1 cm). Heat the oil over medium-high heat until little bubbles begin to form. Check the temperature of the oil by tossing in some bread crumbs; it will be ready when they sizzle. Using a flat, slotted spatula, carry each *mozzarella in carrozza* to the frying pan without breaking it. Slip them into the oil, no more than 2 at a time, and turn down the heat a bit, if necessary, to gently fry the sandwiches. Fry until they are crispy and golden, about 2 minutes on each side. Turn them once, lifting them up with the spatula and using a second spatula on top: Gently squeeze to hold the sandwich together, and let it slide into the oil to fry the other side. Remove the sandwiches from the oil and place on absorbent paper to drain while you fry the others. Serve immediately.

Parmigiana di zucca
PUMPKIN PARMESAN
Serves 6

2 pounds (1 kg) pumpkin, butternut, or similar winter squash

2 eggs

3 tablespoons all-purpose (plain) flour

Salt

2 tablespoons (30 ml) milk (optional)

Extra virgin olive oil, for frying

1 pound (500 g) fresh or canned tomatoes, peeled

10 ounces (280 g) fresh mozzarella, thinly sliced (see Choosing Ingredients)
Freshly ground black pepper
1 cup (125 g) grated Parmesan cheese, plus more for serving

This dish makes a nice vegetarian main course.

Remove the pumpkin's seeds and skin, and cut the flesh in pieces of about 1 inch by 2 inches by ½ inch (2 by 4 by 1 cm). In a bowl, mix together the eggs and flour and a pinch of salt; if it is too thick for dipping add the milk.

Pour oil in a frying pan, estimating an amount that will half cover the pumpkin pieces, and heat over a medium-high flame until little bubbles begin to form. Dip the pieces of pumpkin in the batter and fry them in the oil until they are crisp, about 2 minutes on each side. Keep the oil very hot while you're frying them. Remove them from the oil with a slotted spoon or spatula and drain on absorbent paper.

In a bowl, crush the tomatoes with a fork. Layer one-third of the pumpkin pieces in the bottom of a medium sized baking pan. Cover the pumpkin with half the mozzarella, one-third of the crushed tomatoes, some salt, a little black pepper, and half of the grated Parmesan. Repeat the procedure until you have 3 layers of pumpkin and 2 of filling, and

•

Perfect pumpkins
from Paulo's market garden.

Ugo Calvelli proudly displays the results of a long, morning hunt.

over the last layer of pumpkin put the remainder of the tomato, a little oil, and some pepper. Bake for 20 minutes at 350°F (180°C). This dish will turn out better if prepared ahead of time and reheated in the oven at about 240°F (120°C) just before serving. Serve with additional grated Parmesan.

Stewing

Stewing is casserole cooking, done slowly at a low temperature, and with the cover on the dish in order to lose as little liquid as possible. Usually food thus cooked needs to be browned beforehand and, at the end, it is often necessary to check the thickness of the sauce formed while cooking, and to adjust by either evaporating or diluting it.

Coniglio alle erbe
RABBIT WITH FRESH HERBS
Serves 6

2 tablespoons all-purpose (plain) flour

1 (4-pound or 2-kg) rabbit, dressed and cut into small pieces

2 tablespoons (30 g) unsalted butter

3 or 4 tablespoons (50 to 60 ml) extra virgin olive oil

1 clove garlic, minced

2 teaspoons minced fresh rosemary

2 leaves sage, minced

½ cup (125 ml) dry white wine

Salt

1 cup (250 ml) water

This is to be served as a main course. *Peperonata* (see page 124) makes a good accompaniment.

Put the flour in a shallow dish and dredge the rabbit pieces through it, shaking off excess flour. Put the butter and the oil in a heavy aluminum pan over medium heat and brown the rabbit pieces well on all sides; this should take about 15 minutes. Add the garlic, rosemary, and sage to the well-browned rabbit, mixing with a wooden spoon and taking care that the garlic does not burn. The temperature should be high during this cooking stage. Turning the rabbit and herbs continuously, pour in the wine, and allow it to evaporate almost completely, which should take 5 to 7 minutes. Add a little salt and the water, lower the heat as low as it will go, and cover the pan as tightly as possible with a lid. Cook for about 20 minutes, checking frequently that enough liquid remains so the rabbit won't stick to the bottom of the pan.

When the rabbit is done, it will be tender to a fork and there should be no trace of blood on the bones. Transfer the rabbit pieces from the pan to a serving platter and cover to keep warm while you finish the sauce. The sauce left in the pan should be creamy; if it is too thick, dilute it with water and heat through; if it is too thin, turn the heat up to reduce it. However, keep it a little more fluid than you want, because the flour you used at the beginning will thicken the sauce a lot at the end. Spoon the sauce over the rabbit and serve hot.

Francesina
BOILED BEEF, TOMATO, AND ONION STEW
Serves 6

1 pound (500 g) boiled beef (see page 24)
2 pounds (1 kg) red onions (about 4), thinly sliced
1 cup (250 ml) extra virgin olive oil
2 fresh or canned tomatoes, peeled
Salt
Freshly ground black pepper
1 cup (250 ml) meat stock (see page 24)

This is yet another dish prompted by the need to reuse leftovers. Nevertheless, it is so good that often meat is boiled for the very purpose of obtaining the ingredients for this recipe. It is truly an inexpensive main dish to be accompanied by lots of bread and perhaps Puré di patate (see page 31). I like it a great deal.

Cut the boiled beef in 1-inch-thick (2-cm) cubes. Be prepared to cry when slicing the onions, because this is a lot of onions! But don't worry: the volume will go down substantially with cooking.

Use a heavy cast aluminum baking pan with a wide bottom, 16 inches (40 cm) in diameter with a rim 2 to 3 inches (4 or 6 cm) high (a round oven pan may be used). Pour the oil in the bottom of the pan and add the onions. Put the pan on the stove over medium heat and cook for 20 to 25 minutes, stirring often with a wooden spoon. The onions should wilt first, then stew evenly and lose volume. If you have a lid large enough to cover the whole pan, it will be easier to stew the onions well; otherwise you will have to add ½ cup (125 ml) of water while stirring to keep the onions from burning. When the onions are reduced, raise the temperature to high and brown them long enough to caramelize the sugar they contain, 3 to 4 minutes. When the onions have become a dark brown color (but don't burn them!), add the tomatoes and squash them with a fork. Cook for another 2 or 3 minutes and add a little salt and a lot of pepper. Add the cubes of boiled meat and cover everything with the meat stock. Keep cooking for about 30 minutes, constantly checking the pan and adding stock or water if necessary. If the cooking liquid evaporates, the dish will burn. Serve hot.

Carciofi al tegame
ARTICHOKE AND PROSCIUTTO CASSEROLE
Serves 6

10 or 12 small artichokes
2 ounces (50 g) prosciutto rind, cubed (see Choosing Ingredients)
2 cloves garlic, chopped
1 tablespoon minced flat-leaf parsley
½ cup (125 ml) extra virgin olive oil
Freshly ground black pepper
Salt
½ cup (125 ml) meat stock (see page 24) or water

This is a good example of a stew made with vegetables, which should always be cooked without losing their natural moisture and without adding other liquids, or at least adding as little as possible. The secret to making this an exceptional dish is to put all the raw ingredients into the pan together, adding just a ladle of meat stock, or water if you have no stock. The results with water will not be the same, but good nevertheless. Serve as a side dish, especially with lamb.

Clean and cut the artichokes as described on page 110; however, in this case it is better not to put them in water and lemon, instead just use water, because the lemon may leave a tinge of sourness.

Put the prosciutto, garlic, and parsley into a heavy-bottomed stainless steel pan. (It is better not to use aluminum in this case because the iron in the artichokes may oxidize in contact with aluminum.) Add the quartered artichokes, oil, pepper and, sparingly, salt (the prosciutto is salty). Tightly cover the pan and cook over very low heat, checking often and stirring with a wooden spoon, for about 15 minutes. To check for doneness, probe the artichoke bottoms with a fork and taste a leaf or two; the artichokes should be al dente. Serve warm.

Peperonata
Sautéed Sweet Peppers
Serves 8

Partially cooked Peperonata

½ cup (125 ml) extra virgin olive oil

2 red onions, sliced

2 fresh or canned tomatoes, peeled

Salt

2 pounds (1 kg) bell peppers (capsicums) (about 6 or 7), seeded and cut into 1-inch (2-cm) strips

In season, it is better to use yellow bell peppers in this dish, because they are the sweetest, but red peppers will do. *Peperonata* is served as a side dish, to accompany pork, lamb, or any other fatty meats.

Use a heavy aluminum baking pan with a wide bottom about 16 inches (40 cm) in diameter with a rim 2 to 3 inches (4 to 6 cm) high (a round oven pan may be used). Pour the oil in the bottom of the pan and add the onions. Put the pan on the stove over medium heat and cook for about 20 minutes, stirring often with a wooden spoon. The onions should wilt first, then stew evenly and lose volume. If you have a lid large enough to cover the whole pan, it will be easier to stew the onions well; otherwise you will have to add ½ cup (125 ml) of water while stirring to keep the onions from burning. When the onions are reduced, raise the temperature to high and brown them long enough to caramelize the sugar they contain, 3 to 4 minutes. Be careful not to burn them.

Add the tomatoes and squash them into the onions with a fork. Add a little salt and cook for another 2 or 3 minutes. Add the peppers, and stir for about 20 minutes with the pan uncovered. Add a small quantity of water if necessary to keep the vegetables from burning. The difference in water content between a fresh, meaty pepper, full of its natural juice, and another one, slightly wilted or just left for some time in the refrigerator, is remarkable. The results will be vastly different; because of that I feel unable to give more precise directions than to tell you to add only a little water, only when you need to, with the understanding that the less water added, the better. Add more salt sparingly, and only after tasting. When the peppers are slightly wilted, cover the pan, turn the heat down to low and cook for about 30 minutes. Mind the *peperonata* carefully, turning it frequently, until the peppers are fully cooked and the sauce creamy.

The *peperonata* may be served hot or, in summer, at room temperature, but not refrigerated. It is better if left to stand for a while before serving.

Pot Roasting or Braising

Like the soffritto, pot roasting is a basic procedure for the foundation of many dishes in Italian cooking. It is the indispensable initial stage of casseroles and stews, and of meat-based sauces as well. A careless browning, or indeed a lack of browning, is a bad habit of many hurried cooks, which can reduce a good meat stew to a dish of boiled meat with tomato. The next few recipes have been selected as good examples of the need to master pot roasting.

There was a time when Florentine butchers were really skilled, the best in Italy, and the butcher shops were always full of patrons. It was not uncommon to hear a butcher saying to a young woman, "Oh, good wife, cut it this way, understand?" as he showed the cutting direction with a finger. As a matter of fact, meat joints have a grain. If they are sliced in the wrong direction, the slices will be hard and fibrous, so the basic instruction I give you is to always cut across and not along the muscle fibers.

◆

*Fresh peppers for sale
in the market (above)*

◆

*Butcher Silvano Massi works in
his Florentine shop, which was built
in the late 1800s. (right)*

Roast Beef
TUSCAN POT ROAST
Serves 6

½ cup (125 ml) extra virgin olive oil

2 to 3 pounds (1 to 1½ kg) beef rump, in one piece

½ cup (125 ml) red wine, any variety

Salt

1 teaspoon (5 ml) prepared mustard (optional)

Don't be misled by the English name, which we use in Tuscany. This dish has some similarity to the English pot roast, hence the name, but it is a very different preparation. It is preferably made with *scannello* (rump roast), which gives compact and regular slices. You may also use *bicchiere* (rolled rump roast), which should be tied with a string to keep the slices from splitting along the natural meat cleavage, or *girello* (top round), which is cut from the leg and gives very regular slices, but is less tender than other cuts. Serve as a main course, accompanied by fried potatoes, tomato salad, or *Spinaci saltati* (see page 83).

Choose a pot that is just large enough to contain the joint of meat. Put the oil in the pot, turn the flame to high and brown the roast on all sides, except where it has been cut by the butcher. A good browning means that all sides develop a crust of deep brown color. To determine when you should turn it, lift the meat from the pot; if it sticks to the bottom of the pot, the crust has not yet formed. When the meat is browned, pour in the wine and add some salt. (To ensure a tastier, more consistent gravy, stir the mustard into the wine before you pour it in the pot.) Continue to cook over high heat, turning the meat often, so that each side is immersed in the boiling liquid for about 2 minutes.

The beef must not cook for a long time, since the meat inside must be rare. The exact time will be determined by the size of the joint, but the browning time plus 15 minutes of cooking in wine will probably be sufficient. The beef should be dark brown on the outside, and pink on the inside. Probe with a fork to check for tenderness. Lift the beef out of the pot and set it on a carving board or platter. Check the density of the gravy; if you think it is too liquid, leave it over high heat, stirring with a wooden spoon until it becomes a bit thicker. Taste the gravy for salt: Since it is unlikely that the inner meat will be salty enough because of the short cooking time, the gravy spooned onto each slice has the double task of flavoring and adjusting the saltiness of the meat.

VARIATION WITH LEMON AND ROSEMARY SEASONING

1 tablespoon chopped fresh rosemary
1 strip lemon zest, minced
Salt
Freshly ground black pepper

Another solution to seasoning the meat, especially when cooking a joint larger than 2 pounds, is to stuff the meat. Mince together the rosemary and lemon zest and mix in some salt and a little pepper. Before cooking, make a hole right through the joint with a long, sharp knife and, using the handle of a wooden spoon, push in this seasoning mixture. This is not only a better means of salting the meat, but it also adds some nice complementary flavors. Brown and cook the roast as described on the previous page.

Slice the meat rather thickly and spoon gravy over each serving. The beef can also be kept covered in the refrigerator for up to 2 days and served cold, dressed with good extra virgin olive oil and lemon.

In Tuscany, the finest beef comes from grass-fed Chianina cattle.

Involtini
Rolled Roast of Beef Stuffed with Artichokes and Mortadella
Serves 12

2 large artichokes

3 cloves garlic, minced

3 tablespoons minced flat-leaf parsley

3 pounds (1½ kg) beef thigh or rump, cut in 12 slices

Salt

12 (1 by 2½-inch or 2½ by 6-cm) slices mortadella

⅔ cup (150 ml) extra virgin olive oil

4 fresh or canned tomatoes, peeled

2 bay leaves

Salt

1 cup (250 ml) meat stock (see page 24), or water

This is yet another Florentine dish in which browning is essential. To make it, a slice of beef per person is needed, usually the cuts we call *lucertolo* or *fesa*, from the thigh or rump, which are not stringy but are compact enough to withstand long cooking time. Mortadella are very large sausages from Bologna, made of large pieces of pork, fat, spices, and often pistachios. Serve as a main course, accompanied by *Spinaci saltati* (see page 83).

After cleaning the artichokes (see page 109), cut them lengthwise in 8 segments. Combine the garlic and parsley in a small bowl. Flatten the thin meat slices on a chopping board. Sprinkle a little salt on the upper surface of each slice, lay a mortadella slice on top, and place an artichoke segment over that. Lay the artichoke segment across the mortadella slice. Finally, add a pinch of the garlic and parsley mixture to each.

Now roll the meat around the artichoke segment, beginning from the top and making a roll that you can close with 2 toothpicks. Or you may tie the *involtini* with kitchen string, which will simplify the roasting—just remember to remove the string at the end. Heat the oil in a large, shallow pan over high heat until it begins to bubble. Brown the rolls on all sides, turning them carefully, until they are evenly browned, about 5 minutes. When the rolls are browned, strain the tomatoes through a food mill directly over the pan, and add the bay leaves and a little salt. Keep turning the *involtini* until the tomato thickens a bit, about 5 minutes. Pour in the stock, turn the heat to low, and cover the pan. Cook for 25 to 30 minutes, removing

Involtini

the cover after the first 20 minutes. Throughout the cooking time, check the liquid level to make sure it covers the rolls, and turn the *involtini* often. Serve rolls hot, whole or sliced, covered with the cooking sauce.

Spezzatino
BEEF AND POTATO POT ROAST
Serves 6

1¾ pounds (800 g) beef brisket or other stewing beef
½ cup (125 ml) extra virgin olive oil
2 cloves garlic, sliced
3 or 4 leaves sage
3 fresh or canned tomatoes, peeled
6 to 8 boiling potatoes, about 2 pounds (1 kg), peeled and cubed
Salt
Freshly ground black pepper

This is a poor man's dish, made with the cheapest cuts of meat, especially with the sinewy muscle ends. For several years just after the war ended in Florence it was called *spezzatino del pelliccia* (fur stew), not because it included animal pelts but because of the rhyme of a local bit of doggerel ending with "much potato, but where's the meat?" I prefer that this recipe use more potatoes than meat, but don't go to extremes. It is not difficult to prepare, but without care in browning the meat, the result is not only bad, but revolting. This main dish needs no accompaniment because of the amount of potatoes in it.

Cut the meat in cubes about 1¼ inches (3 cm) across. Put the oil in a large pot over high heat, add the meat, and brown for about 15 minutes. Turn frequently, so that every piece has a crunchy crust all around. When the meat is browned, toss in the garlic and sage and stir with the meat for a few seconds, then add the tomatoes, squashing them with a fork to mix them well with the meat.

Turn the flame to low, cover the pot, and cook for about 20 minutes. Add the potatoes, just cover the ingredients with water, add salt and pepper, and cover the pot. Cook over a low flame for 20 to 30 more minutes, checking both the level of liquid and the saltiness frequently. Remove the braise from the flame and leave it to rest for a while before serving; if left too long, however, the *spezzatino* must be reheated, as it should be served hot.

Aluminum Foil Cooking

This is an excellent cooking method, though it is not suitable for just any type of food. For example, I would strongly suggest that you not cook spaghetti in this way, although I have seen it done in France.

Foil cooking is suitable when short cooking times are required, when no fluids need to be added, and when previous operations such as browning or basic preparations such as a soffritto are not required. With suitable foods, the results are splendid, because the foil enables the food to keep all its natural flavor and moisture. In particular, it is suited for seafood because it enables the kind of gentle cooking that enhances the delicacy of these flavors.

Sgombro all'elbana
MACKEREL ELBA STYLE
Serves 6

3 cloves garlic, peeled
2 cups (50 g) chopped flat-leaf parsley
1 tablespoon chopped fresh rosemary
2 strips lemon zest
1 fresh chile pepper, seeded (see Choosing Ingredients)
Salt
6 mackerel, cleaned and dressed
6 tablespoons extra virgin olive oil

The people who live on the Island of Elba created this recipe to cook mackerel using a chopped mixture of herbs to infuse flavors into the fish. It is difficult to prescribe the quantities for such a mixture of herbs because of the many variables surrounding such a dressing. These include the intensity of the herbs and the preferences of the eaters. For example, it is always a challenge to guess how far one can go in the way of tang, where one may run rampant with the garlic, or where a little chile pepper is not disturbing. I am positive that so far I have respected the basic tastes of Italian cooking; still, your possible objections ring in my ears—"What, all this garlic?!" As my objective is to encourage you to cook and (especially) to eat well, and not to scare you, I never

Rosemary

give mandatory quantities. However, the amounts I give are the right ones for making a recipe for the first time. After that, it is up to you to make adjustments, using my indications as guidelines but going by your own tastes. This is a main course, to be accompanied by tomato salad, green salad, or raw vegetables.

Mince together the garlic, parsley, rosemary, lemon zest, chile pepper, and a little salt. Place a generous teaspoonful of this mixture in the belly of each mackerel, close the fish, and sprinkle a little salt on the outside.

Make 6 double-thick rectangles of foil, 12 by 20 inches (30 by 50 cm); or you may even triple the rectangles, because the fish tail might pierce them. Place a mackerel horizontally in the center of each rectangle, and add I tablespoon of oil to each packet. Fold the foil in over the nose and tail. Seal the top and bottom edges of the foil into the packet, with the seam on top so it remains above the liquids that will cook out of the fish. Cover the bottom of a baking pan with ½ inch (I cm) of water, place the foil packets in the water. Bake at 350°F (180°C) undisturbed for 15 to 20 minutes. I prefer serving the packets still sealed, letting each diner open his or her own; this practice retains the maximum amount of flavor. If necessary, you may help your guests bone and skin the fish.

Cristina and Benedetta
check the consistancy of a Panna cotta.

Bain-Marie

A bain-marie, also called a double boiler, consists of a pan for food that fits into a larger one full of simmering water, heated by direct flame or in the oven. This keeps the cooking food at a steady low temperature, just below the boiling point. In Tuscany, a bain-marie is used mostly for cooking certain cakes based on eggs, which need slow cooking with gentle heat. But it is also very well suited for reheating previously cooked dishes that might be spoiled by direct exposure to flame, such as stews and sauces that could otherwise dry out excessively or separate.

Panna cotta
EGG CUSTARD WITH CARAMEL
Serves 8

1½ cups (300 g) sugar
5 egg yolks, plus 2 whole eggs
2 cups (500 ml) heavy cream

This cooked custard made with whipped cream is an easy-to-make dessert and is widely appreciated, although it requires a rather lengthy cooking time. You may experience some difficulty in taking the *panna cotta* out of the molds, so I suggest using small, disposable aluminum custard molds or ramekins. A good rule is to prepare the caramel needed to line the inside of the molds beforehand. The caramel performs a dual task: While the cream is cooking, it is a protective layer that prevents the cream from touching the hot metal of the mold; and at the end it becomes part of the dessert.

Put two-thirds of the sugar (14 tablespoons or 200 g) into a small pot and place over medium heat. When the bottom layer begins to melt, begin to stir the sugar slowly with a wooden spoon. The sugar will melt gradually, darkening, and soon after it has all melted small bubbles will appear and form a sort of froth on the surface. When the bubbles start to grow in size and the level in the pot begins to rise, take it off the flame. You'll see that the sugar will continue to boil for a while. When it stops, use a small ladle to check that the color is a uniform dark brown, and the caramel is of a smooth and liquid consistency. Off the stove, the caramel becomes denser, and indeed after about 30 seconds it will no

longer be completely fluid. When it has reached this consistency, pour the caramel into a large mold or into single-serving molds, and let it harden into a single, even layer.

Preheat the oven to 225°F (100°C). In a round-bottomed bowl, beat the 5 egg yolks and the remaining sugar with a whisk and, when it is well blended (a yellow, smooth consistency) add the 2 whole eggs. Continuing to whisk, add the cream. Pass the mixture through a fine sieve to eliminate any specks from bits of sugar and egg. Fill up the molds and place them in a deep baking pan. Pour cold water into the pan to about ½ inch (1 cm) below the rims of the molds. Cover the pan with foil and bake for at least 1½ hours, or 2 hours if a large mold is used. Check for doneness by inserting a toothpick. When it comes out dry, the dessert is done. Remove the pan from the oven and take the molds out of the water. Allow the *panna cotta* to cool down for 30 minutes, then cover and refrigerate for at least 2 hours before serving.

To remove the custards from the molds, insert a knife blade at the top, where the custard contacts the mold, enabling the custard to slide out when the mold is turned upside down onto a plate. But if, as sometimes happens, this does not work, heat the bottom of the mold very briefly over boiling water and try again. Chill and serve.

♦

Bonnet

Bonnet
AMARETTO CUSTARD
Serves 12

1 cup (270 g) sugar, plus 3 tablespoons
4 cups (1 l) milk
⅓ cup (75 ml) espresso or doubly-strong coffee
20 coffee beans, coarsely chopped
2 tablespoons powdered cocoa
8 eggs, separated
14 ounces (400 g) amaretti biscuits

For this recipe, you'll need *amaretti*, biscuits made of almonds and egg white. These are widely available in Italian and specialty food stores. If you do not have an espresso maker at home, use the coffee maker you have to brew doubly-strong coffee: Make a pot of coffee, then put new coffee in the filter and use the first pot of coffee in place of water.

Make a caramel lining for the molds following the directions in the recipe for *Panna cotta* (see page 135). You will need to use 1 cup less 2 tablespoons (200 g) of the sugar. Pour the caramel into 2 rectangular molds of about 3 by 8 inches (7 by 20 cm), with sides about 3 inches (7 cm) high.

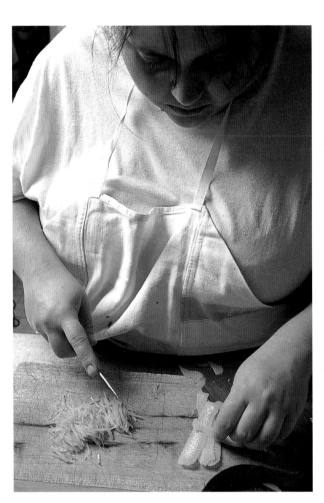

Put the milk, espresso, and chopped coffee beans in a saucepan over low heat. Heat to a simmer, making sure it does not boil or burn. Remove the milk mixture from the heat and allow it to cool. When it is lukewarm, add the remaining 5 tablespoons (70 g) of sugar and the cocoa, stirring them in with a whisk. Strain the milk mixture through a sieve into a large bowl.

Fill a baking pan with enough water to come to ½ inch (1 cm) below the mold rims and put it in the oven without the molds. Preheat the oven to its maximum temperature. While the oven is heating, whip the egg whites until stiff. Fold the egg yolks in with the whites with slow movements from the bottom up. Do this with a spoon, or with your hands, having cooled them under the tap.

Break the *amaretti* up loosely by hand without crumbling them. Now you will mix all the ingredients in the following sequence, moving quickly so the *amaretti* do not become mushy. First put the *amaretti* into the milk and coffee mixture. Then, with care and continuing to mix from the bottom up to keep the whites from going flat, add the egg mixture. Fill up the molds with a ladle a little at a time, trying to distribute the liquid and the froth evenly. As soon as the oven's maximum temperature is reached, put the molds into the hot water bath and bake for 2 or 3 minutes, enough to form a thin crust on the surface of the custards. Immediately lower the temperature to 200°F (90°C) and cover the molds with foil. Cook for 1½ hours. Start probing the custards with a toothpick every few minutes. When the toothpick comes out dry, take the molds out of the oven and remove them from the water bath. Cool the custards for 30 minutes at room temperature and then cover them and chill for a minimum of 2 hours in the refrigerator. Because of its consistency, *bonnet* is no problem to remove from the mold. Just loosen gently with a knife along the top of the custard where it contacts the mold. Put a plate on top and turn it upside down; it will come out easily. Serve chilled.

Cristina fills aluminum molds for Panna cotta (right) and cuts orange zest to garnish desserts (above).

Ragù

ragù

Theme and Variations on Meat Sauces

In the last twenty years or so, the style and presentation of cookbooks have changed dramatically. It is no longer in fashion to simply instruct the diligent housewife. Cookbook authors have always provided recipes, but in addition they used to describe how to serve dishes, how to set the table, how to behave, and many other suggestions that contributed to the "bon ton" of the middle class.

Nowadays almost no one publishes heavy, all-encompassing works dealing with how to prepare coffee, which liqueur must be served to the ladies, how to make a formal soufflé, and so on, whether in regional, national, or international cooking. The huge variety of information available to domestic cooks has quelled the encyclopedic fervor, so that each book may now instead address increasingly specialized types of cooking, with titles such as *How to Cook Lamb in Apulia on Odd Days: Twenty Recipes with Illustrations.* Sometimes I appreciate this specialization and depth of detail. It seems to acknowledge the impossibility of omniscience. For example, quite a few regional recipe books are interesting and useful for consultation, as they focus on the characteristic elements of a particular place, conveying the feeling of the land with its gastronomical history and style.

This evolution in culinary literature points out the changing social and cultural realities of our times. Cookbooks are no longer addressed to someone who sees the kitchen as her primary workplace, but to a generic public, and they give directions that resemble the instruction booklets for electric appliances. The authors? They, too, are altogether different characters. They may not be cooks—they may not even be good eaters. I would call the new breed of cookbook author a researcher or a scholar, neither cook nor gourmet, but better identified as a journalist whose task is to document, classify, and describe. Many cookbook writers today simply do not have enough experience in the market and the kitchen to form strong personal feelings about food. One can still occasionally find cookbooks written by cooks, imparting something of their experience and opinions, but the general trend is toward simple instruction.

Beyond the question of expertise in and passion for the subject, I relish a book whose investigation of food involves a quest for pleasure. There is no point in dealing with food

The grape pickers at Fattoria Corzono & Paterno enjoy a hearty lunch.

if we cannot accept our dependence on it as a source of pleasure or if we are ashamed of or fear criticism for our appetites. Despite the advancement of human knowledge in every field, perhaps the idea of sin still dominates us so much so that we think our pleasure in food is "evil." Many food writers invoke health as a pretext to restrain our natural yearnings toward fulfillment, prescribing dietary prohibitions to relieve us of our sin. I say you should be suspicious of anyone who speaks of eating and doesn't eat, and also of someone who cooks and doesn't eat—something has gone astray there.

Benedetta, Lorenzo, and Armando in Zibibbo's kitchen

Joy, pleasure, delight! Nobody has written a cookbook beginning with these three words, and there are less and less books suggesting that you "cook this dish because it is delicious," extolling above all its ability to satisfy the palate and soul. I have found plenty of dishes praised for their practicality, economy, dietetic qualities, exoticism, and authenticity, yet so few people suggest cooking this or that simply because it is good eating.

Writers should not deny readers the enjoyment of an enthusiastic description of something delicious in the effort to produce rules good for everybody. What can I say? I miss the cookbooks of bygone years, when they were essentially a way to hand down experience.

Why all these protestations? I suppose I am trying to defend myself against the charge that I am crazy for writing this chapter—a whole chapter where the same recipe is given time and again, where the essential idea is to do the same thing over and over. However, I believe that repetition is key to the process of learning.

The repetition in this chapter is not intended to reinforce a series of rote actions. Rather, I want to stimulate in you the acts of judgment that are indispensable in cooking: trying, tasting; trying again, tasting again; evaluating.

I propose, therefore, to start with one classic recipe, which I will give in as much detail as possible. After that, my task is complete, and it will be up to you to experiment and to evaluate the effects of small tricks and subtle variations. It will be you who will achieve better and better results. Having wagged the ladle for twenty years, I am absolutely convinced that if you don't put part of yourself into the pot, all you will have done is to put together some ingredients.

As I have already admitted, I am merely offering some of my personal experiences in the kitchen. Therefore, I have chosen the recipe that has been my own experimental piece. It also has the advantage of being quite a popular dish, so that you may easily compare your own results with those of other cooks.

If you open any Italian cookbook—that is not vegetarian, of course—you'll surely find one or more recipes for meat-based sauces, or *ragùs*. They may be extremely varied; for example, the Neapolitan *ragù* is completely different from the Bolognese one, both in ingredients and in preparation. Nevertheless, a trademark of Italian cooking is the ubiquitous presence of pasta sauces based on meat.

The one I will give first is the "meat sauce" of Florence, which nowadays is truly made of meat, but in the past could have been done with offal and *brincellini* (odds and ends). This is a recipe that, over the years, takes on a very personal character, so much so that my former husband and I, although we cooked together for many years, each make it in a slightly different way.

For these sauces, I insist that you use a suitable pot or pan, considering that both making a soffritto and browning of the meat will always be necessary. Materials are needed that will sustain high temperatures and transmit heat evenly without burning—a very important detail. Cooking vessels made of heavy cast aluminum or tin-plated copper are best. None of the new materials are really able to replace them.

Whichever sauce you decide to make, read through the first recipe in this chapter, as well as the recipe you're going to make. The method of the first version contains some hints that will help you with all of the others (such as how to still make a good sauce even if you discover your meat is mediocre).

All of these *ragùs* are intended as sauces for pasta, to be served as first courses. *Ragù* can also be used with gnocchi and polenta, in lasagna, and risotto (see *Ragù con funghi* page 159). If you use any of these *ragùs* as a sauce for pasta, follow the instructions for cooking and dressing pasta in Chapter I on page 15. *Ragù* (but not cooked pasta) can be kept covered in the refrigerator for up to 2 days and reheated on the stove over low heat just before serving.

Whichever sauce
you decide to make,
read through the first recipe
in this chapter,
as well as the recipe
you're going to make.

The method
of the first version contains
some hints that will help you
with all of the others.

Ragù
BASIC MEAT SAUCE
Serves 8

1¼ pounds (575 g) very good beefsteak, such as sirloin, rib eye (Scotch fillet), or round steak

1 pork sausage, about 4 to 5 ounces (110 to 140 g)

2 chicken livers

2 ounces (50 g) beef suet

1 chicken neck

1 large or 2 small red onions, minced

1 carrot, peeled and minced

1 large or 2 small stalks celery, minced

½ cup (125 ml) extra virgin olive oil

½ cup (125 ml) dry red wine

Salt

2 fresh or canned tomatoes, peeled

About 4 cups (1 l) water

Freshly ground black pepper

1 piece of lemon zest, cut into thin strips

1 pound (500 g) dried pasta

2 to 3 tablespoons (30 to 40 g) unsalted butter, for dressing

1 cup (125 g) grated Parmesan cheese, for serving

The quantities given here will generously dress pasta for eight people, if you are having an informal dinner among friends. Don't overlook the possibility of saving a small amount of it to dress your midnight spaghetti supper for two the following day, which is one of the small pleasures in life.

This recipe requires a visit to a good butcher to get the first five ingredients. Ask the butcher to mince the beef for you, making sure that it is passed through the mincing machine only once to prevent excessive flaccidity. A knife-mincing would be ideal, but it requires time and a certain skill. Also get a fresh pork sausage, 2 chicken livers and a chicken neck, and a chunk of fresh beef suet, cut from where it looks pink.

Back at home, remove the sausage from its casing, and break it into pieces. Chop the livers, and cut the suet into small cubes. Scorch the chicken neck over a flame in order to eliminate any residual hairs. Put all the meats in a bowl and set aside while you prepare the soffritto.

Choose a pot with a diameter of at least 10 inches (25 cm), so that all the meat will fit in a single layer on the bottom of the pan and you will achieve a good browning. Heat the onion, carrot, celery, and oil in the pot over medium heat until the vegetables are dark brown, about 15 minutes. Except for the first few minutes, when it is unlikely to burn, watch the soffritto closely and stir it often with a wooden spoon. If during this time you have something urgent to do and cannot concentrate on the soffritto, pour in a ladleful of

♦

A family-sized bowl of ragù being served in the old kitchen of Villa Picille.

water to keep it cooking for a while without burning, but as soon as the water evaporates, you must devote yourself to the soffritto again.

The person who taught me to make the soffritto for meat sauces used to say, "Toss in the meat an instant before it burns." She kept the spoon in one hand, continuing to stir, and held the meat in her other hand, ready to catch just the right moment. When you see the time is right, throw in the beef, sausage, livers, chicken neck, and suet and keep turning with the wooden spoon, mixing meat and vegetables thoroughly. Turn the flame higher to begin browning the meat. A good browning is essential for the outcome of this sauce, which otherwise will have an unpleasant taste of boiled meat.

The saying is that the meat should "suffer" at this cooking stage. Don't worry; if you are using the right pot and giving it your constant attention, the meat will form a toasted crust, and even if it tends to stick, it will not burn. Brown for about 15 minutes, taking care to turn and brown the chicken neck also. When, from its color and consistency, you judge that the meat is well done, pour in the wine and raise the flame to the maximum. You'll see that the liquid will take the meat crust off the pot bottom and sides; keep stirring until the wine is all but evaporated and the meat begins to fry again.

I daresay that at this stage of preparation you will be enveloped by a very pleasant smell. Don't be seduced into forgetting what you are doing and letting browning turn to burning. In this recipe, you work at full attention, monitoring all operations carefully, as the browning of both the soffritto and the meat should stretch your attention to the maximum. You will need all your senses, including the olfactory one, to prevent disaster.

If the butcher has sold you meat of less than first quality, you will easily see so while browning it, because a lot of water will come out and it will smell not of good roast meat, but sweetish and bland. If this happens, put in some salt while browning, in order to extract as much water as possible from the meat. The results won't be the same as with good meat, but will be acceptable.

Now back to the sauce. When the wine has evaporated, add the tomatoes and squash them with a fork, then stir to combine them with the meat. Add the water (it should cover the meat by about ½ inch or 1 cm). Lower the flame to the minimum and add salt, pepper, and the lemon zest to the pot.

At this point you can relax or go and do other things. It will be enough to keep an eye on the level of the liquid. Occasionally check the sauce for dryness; it should always be creamy, not crumbly and separated. If it becomes too dry, add hot water. The sauce must cook for 2 hours at the very least, on a very low flame. Toward the end of cooking, taste the sauce and adjust for salt. Finally, take the chicken neck out, and separate the meat from the bone with a fork and a knife (an easy operation now that the neck is well cooked); put the meat back again.

This sauce is suitable for dressing various types of pasta, long or short, dry or fresh, including tagliatelle (egg noodles). When the sauce is nearly done, cook the pasta al dente (see page 15). Whatever type of pasta you use, please avoid wasting a good sauce on over-cooked or too-dry pasta. Warm the serving bowl in which the pasta will be dressed and pour a ladleful of sauce into the bottom of the bowl, adding the butter. When you drain the pasta, especially if it is fresh, reserve a small amount of the cooking water, and add it if the pasta and sauce mixture becomes too dry. Put the drained pasta in the warm bowl and add a lot more sauce. Turn the pasta with a fork and spoon in such a way as to blend it well with the sauce. Serve immediately with abundant grated Parmesan cheese.

◆

Now that you have the basic *ragù*, I will give you some variations that, although they use a similar procedure, call for slightly different ingredients and give different results.

Ragù alla bolognese
BOLOGNESE SAUCE
Serves 6

1 large or 2 small red onions, minced
1 large or 2 small stalks celery, minced
1 carrot, peeled and minced
½ cup (125 ml) extra virgin olive oil
2 ounces (50 g) lardo, diced (see Choosing Ingredients)
¾ pound (330 g) beef, minced
¾ pound (330 g) pork loin, minced
½ cup (125 ml) dry red wine
3 or 4 fresh or canned tomatoes, peeled
2 cups (500 ml) milk
About 2 cups (500 ml) water
Salt

In Bologna, and in the whole Emilia-Romagna region, the tradition of first courses is one of the best in all of Italy. Tortellini, cappelletti, lasagne, *passatelli* and all their variations, and many others—all these are popular dishes that are well-known around the world. The *ragù* described below is in the same great tradition. I cannot claim that this is *the* recipe for Bolognese sauce, unique, genuine, and sealed by the authorities' imprimatur. As with so many classic dishes, numerous equally genuine variations exist; if we went strolling through Bologna interviewing cooks, we would probably collect scores of different versions.

The meat to be used for this version is not exactly the same as in the previous recipe. Both the beef and the pork loin should be of the highest quality, and you should have them minced by the butcher (or mince them yourself if you have the necessary implements).

Follow same procedure for *Ragù* (see page 146), starting with a soffritto. Though in this case add the *lardo* a few minutes before the soffritto finishes cooking. In Bolognese sauce, the soffritto has to be brown, but not as dark as in the *Ragù*.

When the soffritto is nicely browned, add the minced meat and follow the same browning procedure as in *Ragù*. When the meat is well-done, add the wine, raise the flame to maximum, stirring until the wine has evaporated. Add the tomatoes and squash them with a fork, then stir to combine them with the meat. Pour in the milk and water (the liquid should cover the meat by about ½ inch or 1 cm). Simmer over a low flame for 2 hours and check occasionally for salt. If the sauce gets too dry while it is cooking (it should be creamy) add some hot water.

This sauce is suitable for use with tortellini, lasagne, and so forth, and also for gnocchi (potato dumplings) and any sort of dried pasta. Because of the presence of milk, it makes a good dressing sauce. See page 15 for tips on cooking and dressing pasta.

Ragù con fegatini di pollo
MEAT AND CHICKEN LIVER SAUCE
Serves 6

1 pound (500 g) beef, minced

10 ounces (280 g) chicken livers

1 large or 2 small red onions, minced

1 large or 2 small stalks celery, minced

1 carrot, peeled and minced

½ cup (125 ml) extra virgin olive oil

½ cup (125 ml) dry red wine

2 fresh or canned tomatoes, peeled

About 4 cups (1 l) water

Salt

Freshly ground black pepper

The difference in preparation between this sauce and the first *ragù* I gave you is really minor, but not the taste, which is very different from any of the other recipes because of the larger amount of chicken liver. As I love liver, I like this sauce a lot. However, because the taste is a little unusual, it might not be appreciated by everyone. As before, have your butcher mince the beef for you. Cut the livers into small pieces on a chopping board, and combine them with the minced beef. When chopping the chicken livers, check carefully for green smears, which indicate that the gallbladder has ruptured. If this is the case, the contaminated liver will have a very bitter taste, so discard any liver with green smears.

Follow the basic procedure for *Ragù* (see page 146) for the rest of this recipe, substituting the liver and minced beef for the other meats. But keep in mind that because of the creamy consistency of the liver, this meat mixture will tend to stick more to the pot's bottom and sides, so be especially vigilant.

This sauce is especially good with tagliatelle, or thin egg-noodle strips. See page 15 for tips on cooking and dressing pasta.

Ragù con bracioline
MEAT SAUCE WITH BEEF CUTLETS
Serves 8

Ingredients from Ragù (see page 146), minus the chicken livers and neck
8 beef rump cutlets, about 3 to 4 ounces (80 to 100 g) each

This sauce is essentially the same as the *Ragù*, minus the chicken livers and neck. You will be cooking the cutlets with the sauce. So read the instructions below for browning the cutlets, then turn to page 146 for the full method.

Begin making the *ragù*, using a very large, heavy cast-aluminum pot. The pot should be large enough to brown the minced beef, the sausage, and the suet together with 8 beef cutlets. Browning all of these meats is not the easiest of operations, so do it carefully, turning 1 or 2 cutlets at a time until all of them are well browned, together with the minced ingredients. When browning is complete, proceed as described on page 146. The cutlets should stay immersed in the cooking liquid throughout the long, slow-cooking, so check this as you check for the sauce's thickness and saltiness.

A Florentine butcher carefully slices meat.

This recipe allows you to prepare a first course and a main course all at once, but to avoid serving a monothematic meal, I would suggest using the cutlets the first day with a side dish (which could be green beans dressed with the same sauce, or spinach). The following day use the sauce to dress pasta—or, if it does not offend you, you may eat both meat and sauce together as one dish.

Ragù con colli ripieni
MEAT SAUCE WITH STUFFED CHICKEN NECKS
Serves 6

4 ounces (110 g) Tuscan-style bread (about ⅛ of a 2-pound loaf),
   crusts removed (see Choosing Ingredients)
2½ cups (600 ml) milk
4 ounces (110 g) beef, minced for stuffing
1 egg
½ cup (65 g) grated Parmesan cheese
Grated nutmeg
2 teaspoons grated lemon zest
Salt
Freshly ground black pepper
2 chicken necks
Ingredients from Ragù alla bolognese (see page 149)

The procedure for this sauce is the same as for *Ragù alla bolognese* (see page 149), with the addition of two boned, stuffed chicken necks. Have your butcher mince the beef and pork, and bone the chicken necks. Start by making the stuffing for the chicken necks.

In a bowl, soak the bread in ½ cup (125 ml) of the milk, then drain the bread in a sieve so that it is not overly soggy. In a separate bowl, put 4 ounces (110 g) of the minced beef, the egg, Parmesan cheese, a little nutmeg, the lemon zest, salt, pepper, and finally the soaked bread. Mix it all thoroughly, using your hands.

Over an open flame, scorch any residual hair off the chicken necks. Spoon half the stuffing mixture into each of the necks, then roll each neck between your palms to eliminate any air pockets in the stuffed cavity. Tie each with a short piece of kitchen string like a balloon and set them aside.

For everything else, follow the same procedure as in *Ragù alla bolognese*, adding the stuffed chicken necks at the same time you begin to brown the remaining minced beef and the minced pork. When the sauce is done, remove the chicken necks, untie them, and cut them into small slices. Put the sliced chicken necks on top of dressed pasta (see page 15), and serve immediately.

Ragù bianco
WHITE RAGOUT
Serves 6

1 large or 2 small red onions, minced

1 large or 2 small stalks celery, minced

1 carrot, peeled and minced

½ cup (125 ml) extra virgin olive oil

1¼ pounds (575 g) boneless chicken breast, minced

10 ounces (280 g) pork loin, minced

¾ cup (175 ml) dry white wine

1 sprig fresh rosemary

4 or 5 leaves sage

2 cloves garlic, peeled

2 fresh or canned tomatoes, peeled

2 cups (500 ml) milk

About 2 cups (500 ml) meat stock (see page 24) or water

◆

*Pork is a main ingredient
in Ragù bianco.*

Among the various sauces, this one is the quickest to make, which is sometimes an unquestionable advantage. The cooking time for this sauce is no more than 40 minutes in all. Including preparation and cooking, it should take at most 1 hour and 20 minutes, so it can be served frequently, without the need to take a day off from work just to make the sauce! The meats should be passed only once through a mincing machine, or minced with a knife.

The usual soffritto of onion, celery, and carrot is prepared, but this time only brought up to a hazel color, less brown than any of the other sauces in this chapter. Heat the onion, celery, and carrot in the oil over medium heat until the vegetables are a light brown, about 10 minutes. As always, remember to stir frequently and pay attention to the soffritto. When it is the proper color, add the chicken and pork. Turn the heat to medium-high and stir the meat and vegetables until the meat is well browned. Add the wine and turn the heat to its maximum, continuing to stir and dislodging the bits stuck to the sides of the pan. When the wine has evaporated, add the rosemary, sage, and garlic (these should all be removed at the end of cooking). Turn the heat down to low. Continue to brown, stirring constantly, for 2 to 3 more minutes, taking care not to burn the garlic. Add the tomatoes and squash them with a fork. Finally, pour in the milk and

stock (the liquid should cover the other ingredients by about ½ inch or 1 cm). Cook for about 40 minutes.

This sauce should used to dress either *maccheroni* (hollow tubes) or *chioccioloni* (snail-shaped pasta). See page 15 for tips on cooking and dressing pasta.

Sugo di coda
VEAL TAIL RAGOUT SERVED WITH GREEN BEANS
Serves 6

1 veal tail or oxtail, cut in 2½ or 3-inch (6 or 7-cm) pieces
⅔ cup (150 ml) extra virgin olive oil, plus 2 tablespoons (130 ml)
¾ cup (175 ml) dry red wine
1 red onion, minced
1 stalk celery, minced
1 carrot, peeled and minced
6 fresh or canned tomatoes, peeled
About 4 cups (1 l) meat stock (see page 24) or water, or a combination
Salt
Freshly ground black pepper
1 pound (500 g) fresh or dried pasta
2 pounds (1 kg) green beans, trimmed
1 white onion, thinly sliced
2 cloves garlic, minced
½ cup minced flat-leaf parsley
1 fresh chile pepper, chopped (see Choosing Ingredients)
½ cup (125 ml) water
1 cup (125 g) grated Parmesan cheese, for serving
Tuscan-style bread, for serving (see Choosing Ingredients)

◆

Armando gathers peppers in Paulo's garden across from Zibibbo.

This recipe is a bit more complex and requires more time to prepare. In return for your efforts, this dish will be a whole dinner in itself. Don't be misled by the cheapness of the ingredients; this is an exceptional dish. I beg you to test it and if possible, despite the long time required, test it again until you become a specialist, so that your friends will ask you to cook it for them. While oxtail may be substituted, veal is better. Outside of Italy, I have seen veal tail in Chinese supermarkets. Make sure that the tail is true veal and not beef, whose strong taste is not appropriate. Veal tail is easy to recognize because it is pink, and smaller. Use the sauce for dressing pasta—I would use *chioccioloni*—or polenta.

Put the pieces of tail in a baking pan with ⅓ cup (75 ml) of the oil and brown them in an oven heated to 400°F (215°C), turning them often, for about 15 minutes. When all of the pieces are well browned, pour the wine into the pan and continue cooking until the wine is all but evaporated. Take the pan out of the oven.

While the veal tail is browning, make the soffritto. Use a heavy cast-aluminum, or tin-plated copper pot large enough to eventually contain the veal tail pieces in a single layer. Heat ⅓ cup (75 ml) of the oil over medium heat. Add the onion, celery, and carrot and sauté, stirring often and watching constantly, until the soffritto is a deep brown, about 20 minutes.

When both the soffritto and the tail are properly browned, put the tail pieces and any juice left in the baking pan into the soffritto pot. Add 4 of the tomatoes and squash them with a fork against the side of the pot. Add the stock, and some salt and pepper (the liquid should cover the other ingredients by ½ inch or 1 cm). Turn the flame down to low, cover, and cook for 1½ hours. When the meat is falling off the bones, the sauce is done. In a serving bowl put enough of the sauce to dress the pasta, and leave the tail in the pot with the remaining sauce. Keep the serving bowl warm.

Now start the pasta (see page 15), and cook the green beans. In a large pot, combine the beans, white onion, garlic, parsley, the remaining 2 tomatoes, some salt, the chile pepper, the remaining 2 tablespoons of oil, and the ½ cup of water. Cover the pot tightly and cook over low heat for about 15 minutes, checking the beans often. Take the pot off the heat when the beans are cooked al dente.

While the pasta is cooking, gently reheat the veal tails and their remaining sauce over low heat, so they are hot when it's time to serve. Drain the pasta when it is cooked al dente, reserving a little of the cooking water. Mix the pasta with the sauce in the warmed serving bowl, adding some cooking water if the pasta and sauce mixture is too dry. Do not add butter when dressing the pasta; this sauce is complete as it is and does not need more fat. Put some grated Parmesan cheese on the table; it is not absolutely necessary in this case, but it never does any harm.

Put the veal tail pieces and their sauce in a large serving dish, and serve hot, with abundant spongy white bread to mop up the sauce. Serve the green beans on the side.

Ragù con funghi
MEAT SAUCE WITH PORCINI MUSHROOMS ON RISOTTO
Serves 6

Ingredients from *Ragù* (see page 146), minus the chicken livers and neck

¼ ounce (20 g) dried porcini (boletus) mushrooms (see Choosing Ingredients)

About 2 cups (500 ml) water

1 pound (500 g) carnaroli or vialone nano rice (see Choosing Ingredients)

3 tablespoons (50 g) unsalted butter

½ cup (65 g) grated Parmesan cheese, for serving

Freshly ground black pepper, for serving

This variation on the basic *Ragù* is nice for making a particular risotto, not only because the sauce goes well with rice, but also to introduce some variety to break the monotony of pasta.

Follow the usual procedure for *Ragù* (see page 146), minus the chicken livers and neck. While the meat is browning, put the porcini in a saucepan with the water and bring it to a boil for about 2 minutes. Remove the mushrooms from the water with a slotted spoon, and when they are cool enough to handle, chop them coarsely. Filter their blanching water through a cloth napkin or clean kitchen towel to eliminate any dirt. When adding the tomatoes to the sauce, also add the mushrooms, and their blanching water, completing cooking on a very low fire as always.

If the pot in which the sauce is being prepared is not large enough, transfer the sauce to one that can contain the rice as well. Separately, put water to boil. Heat the sauce again to the boiling point, add the rice without stirring it in and cover it with the boiling water by about ½ inch (1 cm). Turn the heat to low and leave uncovered. Let the rice absorb all the added water, undisturbed, for about 10 minutes. It may be necessary to add more water to complete cooking, so make sure you always have some boiling water on hand. When you think it's ready, stir with a wooden spoon and taste to check both doneness and salt. It should be cooked, but still firm. Turn the heat off, cover the pot, and let the rice finish cooking for about 3 to 4 minutes. When the rice is al dente, blend in the butter, and cover the pot for another 5 minutes before serving. Grated Parmesan cheese and pepper should be available at the table so everyone can complete dressing to taste.

Ragù di piccione
SQUAB RAGOUT
Serves 6

½ cup (125 ml) extra virgin olive oil

1 yellow onion, minced

2 small squab (about 7 ounces or 200 g each), plucked, drawn, and cut into 4 pieces

2 bay leaves

1 sprig fresh rosemary

½ cup (125 ml) dry white wine

3 fresh or canned tomatoes, peeled

Salt

Freshly ground black pepper

1 to 1½ cups (250 to 375 ml) meat stock (seee page 24) or water

◆

This pigeon has already chosen his pot.

Heat the oil over medium heat in a heavy cast-aluminum pan and cook the onion for 2 to 3 minutes, until it begins to take on a little color. Add the pieces of squab, the bay leaves, and the rosemary. Turn the squab pieces often until they have reached a beautiful golden color and the onion is not too dark, about 15 to 20 minutes. Pour in the wine, turn the heat to high, and cook, stirring frequently, until the wine is completely absorbed. Now add the tomatoes, and crush them with a fork against the bottom of the pan. Add some salt and pepper, and most of the stock. Cook for approximately 30 minutes over medium heat, adding stock or water from time to time if the sauce becomes too dry and crumbly. The squab is ready when tender. Turn off the heat and remove the squab from the pot to cool. When it is cool enough to handle, remove the bones. Cut the birds in small pieces and put their meat back in the sauce. Remove the bay leaves and rosemary.

Toss this sauce with pasta (see page 15) as you normally would, except do not serve with grated Parmesan.

Layering
Flavors

layering flavors

Who says that a prosciutto roll is no good? Give me good bread and good prosciutto and I'll show you that it is very good indeed. In fact, with a little care and attention, it can be excellent. Warm a fresh roll a little in the oven and lay the prosciutto on top and you will have an exceptional snack. All you must do is avoid buying either a horrible prosciutto unworthy of the name (made with shabby pork, excessive polyphosphates, gas curing, and so many other so-called improvements) or bread produced to have a long shelf life rather than to be enjoyed.

Combining flavors with care is as important a part of food preparation as the greatest cooking techniques. Anyone who has tried a platter of pears and pecorino (sheep cheese) will agree. Pecorino and pears is an example of one of the most successful combinations, where two simple tastes, put together without any elaboration, produce a third, extraordinary flavor.

Consider a submarine sandwich with a lot of fillings inside, well chosen and well matched. Or take a good beef carpaccio and build a meal around it by adding Parmesan cheese, mushrooms, and arugula (rocket). Each of these combinations can be excellent. This, however, cannot be considered cooking. Nevertheless, it is no detraction from the enjoyment of eating an apple, a peach, a good salad, or even that very prosciutto roll to say that cooking is a different kettle of fish. Cooking involves the modification of the primary ingredients through the application of heat or other procedures, thus producing something different from the original food.

In this chapter, I offer a series of recipes based on the search for tastes to assemble and mix, with the aim of finding unusual and interesting combinations.

♦

At I Fratellini (Little Brothers) established in 1875, Florentines enjoy eating Panini al proscuitto sandwiches and sampling wines (left); the tiny cafe has no tables so patrons eat their food in the street (above).

Sauces

I think it apt to start with a range of sauces to be used in various ways: to spread on sandwiches, or to accompany meat dishes, raw vegetables, or whatever else you may fancy. Sauces are often used as a sort of joker—a culinary wild card to trump whatever bland, packaged foods they are made to cover. But when they're carefully paired with truly good foods, the results can be wonderful.

Maionese
MAYONNAISE
Yield: about 2½ cups (625 ml)

6 egg yolks
Salt
1½ cups (375 ml) extra virgin olive oil
Juice of 1 to 1½ lemons

•

Maionese served on a chicken salad.

First, let me give you a recipe for the classic and popular mayonnaise. It is used in hundreds of ways, including as a spread on bread for sandwiches. I make it by hand, using eggs and extra virgin olive oil, and I notice the surprise of some of the patrons of my restaurant when they taste real mayonnaise. Nowadays the expected taste is that of commercially-produced mayonnaise, which is not even a distant cousin of true mayonnaise. The problem with making mayonnaise is that sometimes—and seemingly without reason—it goes crazy; it de-emulsifies, so that you have to start again from the beginning. Don't let this prospect deter you. This sauce is used with seafood, cold meat and chicken, and raw vegetables. It can be kept, well covered, in the refrigerator, for up to 2 days.

Put the egg yolks in a bowl with a pinch of salt and beat them with a wire whisk for about 30 seconds until they become light yellow and smooth. Add the oil in a slow trickle, whisking it into the egg yolks until the sauce starts to thicken. (As you do this, face the mayonnaise and, as convincingly as you can, tell it to behave.) Always move the whisk in the same direction, trying to keep an even pace, which must not be brisk, but slow and uninterrupted. Keep adding the oil in an increasing flow and beating until the mayonnaise is dense enough that the whisk remains standing in it. Taste for salt; if more is needed, dissolve it in the lemon juice, which is the last ingredient to be whisked into the mayonnaise.

Salsa verde
GREEN SAUCE
Yield: about 2 cups (500 ml)

1 large bunch flat-leaf parsley, about 7 ounces (200 g), stemmed

2 or 3 cloves garlic, peeled

4 tablespoons (100 g) capers in vinegar, drained

3 salted anchovies, boned and rinsed (see page 116)

1 teaspoon ground chile pepper (see Choosing Ingredients)

1½ cups (375 ml) extra virgin olive oil

This sauce is a classic of Tuscan cooking and was invented to go with boiled meat. Of the many versions, I will give you the one I like most.

With a knife or *mezzaluna*, chop the parsley together with the garlic. When the parsley and garlic are partially chopped, add the capers and anchovies and mince everything together. When the mince is fine and even, place it in a bowl and add the chile pepper. Stirring constantly, add oil until the mixture is well blended and begins looking like a sauce. Taste; usually it's not necessary to add salt.

Aglioli
GARLIC MAYONNAISE
Yield: about 2 cups (500 ml)

6 egg yolks

Salt

1½ cups (375 ml) extra virgin olive oil

1 clove garlic, minced

2 teaspoons minced flat-leaf parsley

½ teaspoon ground chile pepper (optional) (see Choosing Ingredients)

Juice of 1 to 1½ lemons

It is easy to see that mayonnaise is amenable to further elaboration to suit particular dishes. *Aglioli* is commonly suggested for seafood, but it is also good with boiled meat; it can be kept in the refrigerator, well covered, for up to 2 days.

•

Fresh capers

Put the egg yolks in a bowl with a pinch of salt and beat them with a wire whisk for about 30 seconds until they become light yellow and smooth. Add the oil in a slow trickle, whisking it into the egg yolks until the sauce starts to thicken. Always move the whisk in the same direction, trying to keep an even pace, which must not be brisk, but slow and uninterrupted. Keep adding the oil in an increasing flow and beating until the *aglioli* is dense enough that the whisk remains standing in it. Whisk in the garlic and parsley and, if a hot, spicy taste is desired, some crushed dried chile pepper. Taste for salt; if more is needed, dissolve it in the lemon juice, which is the last ingredient to be whisked into the *aglioli*.

Salsa maltese
MALTESE SAUCE
Yield: about 2 cups (500 ml)

6 egg yolks
Salt
1½ cups (375 ml) extra virgin olive oil
¼ cup (60 ml) white wine vinegar
½ teaspoon sweet paprika

This sauce was born to dress asparagus, though it is also good with cold boiled cabbage or broccoli. It is nothing but a mayonnaise (see page 166) flavored with some sweet paprika, and with white wine vinegar instead of lemon juice. When you serve asparagus, also give your guests the option of eating it dressed simply with extra virgin olive oil and lemon. And please, serve the asparagus al dente, gently retrieving it from the water when it is still a bit crisper than you want, remembering that the inner heat will keep it cooking for a few more minutes. Like all other oil-based sauces, this one can be kept for up to 2 days, no more, well covered, in the refrigerator.

Put the egg yolks in a bowl with a pinch of salt and beat them with a wire whisk for about 30 seconds, until they become light yellow and smooth. See the mayonnaise recipe (page 166) for more details. Add the oil in a slow trickle, whisking it into the egg yolks until the sauce thickens to the density of heavy cream. Slowly add the vinegar and paprika, whisking it into the sauce until smoothly incorporated.

OIL-BASED SAUCES

Many people mistakenly think the oil preserves these sauces, believing that oil is a preservative in itself. Because the oil prevents air from coming into contact with the food, they believe that it will keep the sauce good for days on end. I entreat you, don't believe it. Keep oil-based sauces for no more than two days in the refrigerator. Many people don't realize that some of the most dangerous microorganisms are anaerobic; that is, they develop only in the absence of air, and this can happen to sauces if they are kept too long.

Cold Dishes

Insalata russa
RUSSIAN SALAD
Serves 6

2 beets (beetroots) (optional)

2 or 3 boiling potatoes, peeled

4 carrots, peeled

¾ pound (330 g) green beans

4 medium or 6 small zucchini (courgettes)

14 ounces (400 g) canned tuna packed in oil, drained and cut into pieces

1½ cups (375 ml) Mayonnaise (see page 166)

3 or 4 tablespoons (50 to 60 ml) white wine vinegar (optional)

Basil leaves, for garnish (optional)

3 or 4 ounces (75 to 100 g) peperoni sotto aceto (roasted red and yellow peppers in vinegar),
for garnish (optional)

Despite, or perhaps because of its name, this dish is fairly popular in Tuscany. It is, as you'll see, a salad suitable for the summertime, when it can be served as an appetizer or even, because it contains tuna, as a main course. Let us prepare it thinking of it as a main dish. The addition of red beets is a subject of controversy: The classic recipe includes them, no doubt the legacy of the dish's Russian origins, but indeed they bring to the dish a sweetish taste not appreciated by everybody (including myself, who would rather have it without).

Begin by boiling the vegetables until they are tender, but still firm. This will take different amounts of time for each vegetable. Cook the beets alone, otherwise they will discolor all the other vegetables. Boil the beets for about 30 minutes. Boil the potatoes and the carrots together in the same pot for about 20 minutes. In another pot, boil the beans for about 5 minutes then add the zucchini and keep cooking both for another 10 minutes.

Drain the cooked vegetables, and let them cool down enough to handle. Cut them into cubes, rounds, or slices, according to their original shapes, trying to obtain small and even sized pieces (for example, cut the potatoes in cubes ½ inch or 1 cm across, and the other vegetables to match). Put them in a mixing bowl with the tuna.

◆

A Tuscan delicacy, Ouvli mushrooms
are prized for their delicate flavor
and texture.

Pour a third of the mayonnaise into the bowl and mix the lot well with your hands or a wooden spoon. Taste and, if you like, add a little of the white wine vinegar to lighten the taste and the texture of the tuna and potatoes, which is often rather heavy.

Invert the salad onto a serving plate. Smooth the upper surface of the salad and cover it with the remaining mayonnaise in an even layer. Decorate the top with whatever you like; basil leaves or strips of roasted red and yellow peppers in vinegar are suitable. Put the salad in the refrigerator until about 10 minutes before you serve it.

Vitello tonnato
VEAL WITH TUNA SAUCE
Serves 6

1½ pounds (650 g) girello (boneless veal top round), in one piece
1 red onion, peeled and halved
1 carrot, peeled
2 stalks celery
11 ounces (300 g) canned tuna packed in oil, drained and chopped
3 tablespoons (75 g) capers in vinegar, drained, plus 1 tablespoon for garnish
2 salted anchovies, boned, rinsed, and chopped (see page 116)
1 whole egg, plus 3 yolks
1 cup (250 ml) extra virgin olive oil
Juice of 2 lemons
Salt
1 lemon, thinly sliced, for garnish

This cold dish is suitable for both summer and winter. It is meat-based, but the abundant sauce is a main component. It is easy to make, and, as the old saying goes, it performs well: This dish, when ready, looks like a fairly large amount of food even if the amount of ingredients is not so large. The eyes are easily deceived. Typically, veal is used, but this dish may be made with a good cut of beef, and if an attractive presentation is sought, choose a regular cut such as *girello,* the upper leg cut from which veal cutlets are made. This dish is a main course; a tomato salad is a good accompaniment.

Set a large, covered pot of water over high heat, and when it boils, take off the cover and put in the veal along with the onion, carrot, and celery. Simmer over medium heat for about 45 minutes. The veal is done when it is tender to a fork. Remove from the heat and drain. Discard the vegetables, unless you would like to try the variation below. Allow the veal to cool to room temperature.

In order to demonstrate that I am not a manual-tools-only fundamentalist, I suggest this time that you use a food processor or powerful blender to make the sauce. Combine the tuna, all but 1 tablespoon (25 g) of the capers, the anchovies, egg and egg yolks, oil, and lemon juice in the bowl of a food processor and process to obtain a sauce that is as smooth as possible.

When the meat is completely cold, cut it in slices as thin as possible. Lay the slices on a serving platter without overlapping them, and cover them completely with the sauce. As a garnish, use the reserved capers and very thin lemon slices. Any surplus of sauce may be put in a sauceboat on the table, for anyone who might like more.

VARIATION WITH VEGETABLES

A different version, more delicate but still just as good, calls for the addition of two of the vegetables used for cooking the meat to the sauce ingredients. If you would like a more delicate sauce, blend the boiled carrot and celery into the sauce (you can use the ones you boiled with the veal). Check for salt and add a little if necessary.

Insalata di fegatini
CHICKEN LIVER SALAD WITH GREEN BEANS AND ALMONDS
Serves 6

12 chicken livers
2 cloves garlic, coarsely chopped
6 leaves sage
½ cup (125 ml) extra virgin olive oil, plus more for dressing
Salt
4 ounces (100 g) almonds
1½ pounds (650 g) green beans, trimmed
2 tablespoons (30 ml) white wine vinegar, for dressing
Balsamic vinegar, for dressing

I have confessed already to being a liver-lover. I eat it cooked in any manner, and even raw, as called for in some Korean recipes. Therefore I dedicate this recipe to my fellow liver-lovers, particularly because there is no point in offering liver to liver-haters. Provide one liver per person if you serve this dish as an appetizer, or two if you make a main course of it, as we do here.

Examine each liver for the greenish smears that indicate the gall bladder has burst, and discard any that you find. Cut each liver in half and put in a pan with the garlic, sage, oil, and just a little salt. Sauté over high heat for about 5 to 6 minutes, until the livers become crunchy on the outside. Then turn the heat off and leave the livers in the pan for another 5 minutes. One of the difficulties in cooking liver is to find the exact point of doneness. The cooked liver must not contain blood, but it will be ruined by overcooking, because it gets hard and tasteless. Ideally the inner part should be evenly pink, while a thin crust has formed on the outside.

If your almonds are not already peeled, toss them in boiling water for a few seconds, then drain them, and while they're still hot, peel off the thin brown skin with your fingertips. Now slice the almonds, a task requiring some skill. Place 5 or 6 at a time on a chopping board, on their flat sides. Keeping the almonds steady with one hand, rest the tip of a sharp knife on the board and slice the almonds by moving the handle up and down. Don't worry if the results aren't too impressive the first time. Put the sliced almonds in a pan in a hot oven for a few minutes to toast them a little.

In a large pot, put enough salted water to cover the beans and bring it to a boil. Add the beans and cook uncovered for about 15 minutes, until they are tender, but still firm. Drain and allow them to cool to room temperature.

At this point you may begin composing and dressing. I say composing on purpose, because in this case, mixing all the ingredients together with the dressing is not the suitable way of serving this salad. Carefully place equal portions of green beans and liver on each of six plates, being careful not to break the beans or mash the liver. Sprinkle toasted almonds over each serving, and dress in this order: First with a sprinkling of oil, then white wine vinegar, and finally 2 drops of balsamic vinegar.

A flavorful lunch takes shape on the kitchen counter.

Memory
and
Innovation

memory and innovation

FINDING THE EQUILIBRIUM

All the world's misfortune comes from biting an apple. Luckily, we don't really know what we have lost. Perhaps we should be grateful to He who punished us for sparing us the torture of the constant vision of a paradise lost forever. Anyway, here we are, in this "vale of tears". Even now I cannot fully forget this expression that pestered me as a teenager, trying to see something through the tears.

I have always been attracted to the place around which food, sex, sin, desire, and guilt revolve. I am fascinated to see how our deepest feelings are ruled by the dynamic equilibrium among these elements. What can we do if not try to balance the extremes of goodness and desire? The more we keep the distances equal, the saner we are. I don't believe that human evolution naturally tends toward goodness; I do believe that the motion induced by the competing forces of our nature will not and must not ever stop. And I believe that reflecting upon our struggles and respecting all parts of ourselves is necessary to our well-being.

Why have I indulged in such philosophical thoughts on universal matters, when the theme of this chapter—finding a proper balance between tradition and innovation in cooking—does not really require it? Perhaps because I feel that balance in cooking is but a part of a larger need for harmony in our lives.

I have seen too many people in the last few years who cook or write about cooking who seem obsessed with the exterior look of dishes, with image rather than substance. They seem driven to astonish, to create something visually imposing or intriguing that has little if anything to do with the way the food satisfies the other senses. I have visited restaurants in Los Angeles where the experience was more like watching a theatrical performance than having dinner. It is easier to become popular through magazine pages filled with marvels and abstruse innovations, than by cooking a balanced and well-prepared dish, attractive for no other reason than because it is good and appetizing.

◆

Benedetta, age four, and her family enjoy a roadside picnic. (above)

◆

Nicoletta arranges fruit near the Zibibbo entrance. (left)

It is also true that food sometimes plays an important symbolic or ceremonial role: It has always been associated with hospitality, and its quantity and quality at a banquet can dazzle. While this role is not new, what is new, and not acceptable to me, in these years of fashion-food, is the pecking order of the values, in which visual splendor is all and the food itself is given the least and last position.

One may speculate about the reasons behind a restaurant's serving a risotto decorated with a leaf of gold foil, or why cooks stuff clams with pork, or a pig with clams. Is it motivated by genuine desire to experiment, to apply new techniques, to open new culinary horizons, or is it done simply to show off? As someone who loves eating and who cooks food to be eaten, it disturbs me when those who take up this image-first approach to cooking deny whatever traditions existed earlier, dubbing them obsolete and trivial.

Such an attitude supposes a large gap between the so-called "old" and "new" cuisines, which is absolute nonsense. To me, the best food combines elements of yesterday, today, and tomorrow, reflecting both tradition and innovation. Memory reminds us of our lifelong relationship with food, sentimental and significant. Invention flows from the instinct to discover, to learn, to expand, and even to conform to changing circumstances. Why this principle should be enhanced while memory is denied, I cannot understand. I suggest it is a vital responsibility of all those who would aspire to culinary leadership to fulfill their diners' needs for both tradition and innovation, striking an appropriate balance between the two.

♦

Benedetta (standing) and her brother, Luca (seated at head of table), with friends at a birthday lunch.

With this is mind, I present the recipes in this chapter in a progressive sequence. They are meant to show the process by which classic Tuscan dishes have evolved into different ones. The updated versions are not necessarily better or worse than those that came before; they simply extend the cook's range of options and satisfy requirements we have today that differ from those of the past. This process has been going on for many generations, and, as a chef in this tradition, I am part of the process myself.

Dishes devised in periods of famine, when the primary concern was merely to eat somehow, may be updated to focus on the enjoyment of flavor and taste. In other instances, the aim is to adapt more sophisticated and good-looking dishes for everyday preparation.

My purpose is to illustrate an approach to creative cooking, that maintains the old while incorporating the new. So I give you the recipes in their original versions, their new variations, and, sometimes, their intermediate solutions.

Ravioli
TUSCAN RAVIOLI
Serves 6

1 pound (500 g) spinach, stemmed

1½ pounds (650 g) ricotta

7 eggs

1 cup (125 g) grated Parmesan cheese

Pinch of grated nutmeg

Salt

4¼ cups (600 g) all-purpose (plain) flour

In Italy it is common to confuse the meaning of the word *ravioli*, so that you may order the same dish in the North and in the South and be served something completely different, even in shape. This recipe applies to ravioli made the traditional way in Tuscany, which are shaped as large tortellini stuffed with ricotta and spinach. These are typically served as a first course.

Put ½ inch (1 cm) of slightly salted water in a pot over high heat. When the water boils, toss in the spinach, stir with a wooden spoon, and boil for 2 to 3 minutes. Drain thoroughly, leaving the spinach in the colander for about 10 minutes. Gently press out any excess water with the back of a fork, and mince the spinach as fine as you can. In a bowl, mix the ricotta, spinach, 1 egg, Parmesan cheese, nutmeg, and a little salt. Set aside this filling while you make the pasta.

On a large, flat, smooth surface, put the flour in a ring-shaped heap, and break the remaining 6 eggs into the center. Knead the dough energetically for about 15 minutes until it becomes smooth and elastic. If at any time during the kneading, the dough becomes too hard to knead, add just a little water. If it is wet enough to stick to your hands, add more flour.

Now roll out the dough, not an easy operation if done by hand. Unless you grew up in a household where dough was rolled daily, you will probably not be able to properly roll out the dough with a rolling pin. The sheet of dough must be of even thickness all over, and no thicker than ¹⁄₁₆ inch (2 mm). I suggest using a little contrivance that makes the task much easier: the kind of pasta machine that has two parallel cylinders to flatten the dough and is operated with a hand crank. Using the machine's instructions, feed pieces of your dough into the machine in such a way as to obtain strips of thin dough about 2½ inches (6 cm) wide. Lay the dough strips on a flat surface and cut off any irregular ends. Starting about 1 inch (2½ cm) in from one end of each strip, place spoonfuls of filling (each about the volume of a walnut) every 2½ inches (6 cm) along the strip. With a knife, cut the strips into squares of about 2½ inches (6 cm) on each side, each with a lump of filling in its center.

Fold each square in half diagonally, forming a triangle. The dough at the edges should stick together easily; if it doesn't, wet the edges slightly. Pinch the corners at either end of the base of the triangle. Hold the triangle in one hand and align the index finger of your other hand along the base. Wrap the triangle all the way around your fingertip, forming a ring, and pinch the apex of the triangle to its base. This is the classic shape of tortellini. As you finish forming each piece of ravioli, place it on a platter or board, making sure to leave space between the pieces so they do not stick together.

Boil the ravioli in abundant salted water for only a few minutes, perhaps 3 to 4. Taste one of them to check if the thickest part of the pasta—the sealing at the corners—is cooked al dente. Never toss them into a colander, but retrieve them from the water with a skimmer. They may be dressed with a meat sauce, or simply with melted butter and grated Parmesan cheese.

Gnudi
Serves 6

1 pound (500 g) spinach, stemmed
3 cups (750 ml) Pomarola (fresh tomato sauce) (see page 13)
1¾ pounds (800 g) ricotta
3 eggs
Pinch of grated nutmeg
¾ cup (100 g) all-purpose (plain) flour
¾ cup (100 g) grated Parmesan cheese

Gnudi is the Tuscan dialect word for "naked," which basically means they are ravioli without the "clothing" of pasta. The advantage is that they are much quicker to make because no dough is required, but this creates some problems as to the consistency of the mixture, which must neither fall apart when put into boiling water, nor be so stiff that it becomes hard when cooked. Here is the traditional way to make *gnudi* in Florence.

The quantities are approximate because the consistency of the mixture must be evaluated while preparing it. It depends on quite a few variables—the quality of the ricotta, the amount of water retained by the spinach, the glueyness of the eggs, and so forth. This is a first course.

Put ½ inch (1 cm) of slightly salted water in a pot over high heat. When the water boils, toss in the spinach, cover, and let cook about 3 minutes. Drain thoroughly, leaving the spinach in the colander about 10 minutes. Gently press out any excess water with the back of a fork, and mince the spinach as fine as you can. Heat the tomato sauce in a saucepan over a low heat.

Before you proceed, make ready both the cooking water and the serving bowl for the *gnudi*; you must be able to move straight from forming to cooking to serving the *gnudi*. Set a large pot of salted water on to boil, and put a layer of tomato sauce in the bottom of a warmed serving bowl for the *gnudi*. Keep the serving bowl warm in a low oven while you make the *gnudi*, and keep the rest of the sauce warm, too.

In a bowl, mix the ricotta, spinach, eggs, nutmeg, and begin adding the flour. Mix well, using your hands, adding flour until you can form it into balls the size of a big walnut by rolling the mixture between the palms of your hands. If the balls do not hold together, add more flour in small amounts as necessary, just until the balls hold together. You want the balls to hold together using the least possible amount of flour, so that the *gnudi* will melt in the mouth.

As you finish the balls, lay them on a board or platter covered with a dusting of flour. Sprinkle all their surfaces with a bare coating of flour. Put about 10 *gnudi* at a time into the boiling water, and retrieve them with a skimmer when they come to the surface, after about 1 minute. Remove them with a slotted spoon or a skimmer and allow the water to drop off of them before placing them in the prepared serving bowl. When a single layer is set in the bowl, add some more warm sauce and some grated Parmesan cheese, and so on as soon as each batch is cooked. Don't turn the *gnudi* in the bowl to dress them better, or they will break, and be gentle in serving them. Serve immediately.

Sformato di spinaci
SPINACH SOUFFLÉ
Serves 8

4½ pounds (2¼ kg) spinach, stemmed

1 pound (500 g) ricotta

3 eggs

1 cup (125 g) grated Parmesan cheese, plus more for serving

Pinch of grated nutmeg

1 cup (250 ml) extra virgin olive oil

Salt

1 cup (250 ml) Pomarola (fresh tomato sauce) (see page 13), warmed

This soufflé is so good that any amount of toil would be rewarded when you serve it to your grateful guests. Luckily, it's also quite simple to make, so you can save your toil for another day. This is my own version of this dish, lighter and easier to make than the traditional method. You can serve it as an appetizer, a first course, or an accompaniment to any main dish.

Put ½ inch (1 cm) of slightly salted water in a pot over high heat. When the water boils, toss in the spinach, and boil for 3 minutes. Drain thoroughly, leaving the spinach in the colander for about 10 minutes, squeezing out any excess water.

Mince the spinach and combine it with the ricotta, eggs, Parmesan cheese, nutmeg, and oil in a deep bowl. Beat the mixture with an electric beater at medium speed until it has the consistency of thick yogurt, then taste and adjust for salt. Pour the mixture into a square or rectangular baking pan (about 8 by 8 by 2 inches or 24 by 24 by 6 cm) and smooth the upper surface with a spatula. Bake at 300°F (150°C) for 10 to 15 minutes until the surface is firm and the mixture inside is still uncooked. At this point, cover the pan with foil as tightly as possible and put it back in the oven. After about 10 minutes, uncover and check to see if the soufflé has started rising; if so, cover it again; if not, remove the foil. In either case, lower the temperature to 210°F (100°C) and continue cooking for about 30 minutes.

Shortly before the soufflé is done, spoon some warm tomato sauce over the bottoms of 8 warmed individual serving plates. The soufflé is done when it is firm, but still a bit soft. Remove it from the oven, and take out a strip of about ¾ inch (2 cm) from one side of the pan, using a square spatula. Then, still with the square spatula, cut the soufflé into

♦

Sformato di spinaci

8 equal rectangles. Use the space you created at one end of the pan to ease the spatula under the first rectangle, then lift each serving out, placing another spatula on top to steady it, and slide it onto a serving plate.

Add abundant grated Parmesan cheese to the side of each plate and serve immediately.

Cardi al latte
CARDOONS WITH MILK
Serves 6

2¼ pounds (1½ kg) cardoons (see Choosing Ingredients)
1 cup (250 ml) milk
1 cup (250 ml) meat stock (see page 24) or water
1 whole clove
¼ stick cinnamon
Pinch of grated nutmeg
Salt
7 tablespoons (100 g) unsalted butter
1 cup (125 g) grated Parmesan cheese, plus more for serving
Freshly ground black pepper, for serving (optional)

For those who fancy ancient recipes, this one comes from a Renaissance cookbook. Apart from the inescapable toil of cleaning the cardoons, it is fairly simple. The car-doon—*cardo* in Italian—is a Mediterranean vegetable closely related to the artichoke, of which only the stalks are used. This is a winter dish, as the cardoons, like many other winter vegetables, have to be exposed to cold weather to be tender. There is no substitute for cardoons in this dish, so if you find them in the market, bring them home and enjoy them in this dish or the next one. Serve this as a side dish to a main course; it's especially good with hot boiled meat (see page 24).

To prepare the cardoons, remove any tough outer stalks and cut the inner stalks into 2 to 3-inch (5 to 7-cm) pieces. "Unthread" the cardoons by picking out the strings in the pieces (they are something like the strings in celery stalks) either with your fingers or with a paring knife. To avoid blackening your fingers with the hard-to-remove dye, keep half a lemon handy and rub it frequently on your fingers.

Put the cardoons into a stainless steel pot and cover them by about 1 inch (2 cm) with the milk and stock. Add the clove, cinnamon, nutmeg, and a little salt. Cook, uncovered, over low heat for about 30 minutes, stirring from time to time with a wooden spoon (always use a wooden spoon to stir vegetables). During slow cooking there is often the risk that the cooking liquid will evaporate, so check frequently and if the liquid gets too low to cover the cardoons, add a little stock or water to cover. Once you are used to working in the kitchen, this checking becomes a habit, a task done not just for practical reasons, but also to communicate to the food in the pot that we have not forgotten it.

When the dish is done cooking, the milk will have curdled and reduced to a sort of bubbly cream and the cardoons will be soft and tender. Remove the clove and cinnamon stick. Add the butter and grated Parmesan cheese, and mix well. This dish does not suffer if prepared ahead of time and then reheated gently in a bain-marie (see page 135)—in fact, it gets tastier. Provide your guests with a pepper mill in working order.

Sformato di cardi
CARDOON SOUFFLÉ
Serves 6

2 stalks cardoon (see Choosing Ingredients)
7 tablespoons (100 g) unsalted butter
2 tablespoons all-purpose (plain) flour
2 cups (500 ml) milk
Salt
1½ cups (185 g) grated Parmesan cheese, plus more for serving
2 egg yolks
Freshly ground black pepper, for serving (optional)

Cardoons

This recipe requires the tedious cleaning of the cardoons, but it makes an excellent dish, especially for those who appreciate the cardoon's bitter taste. Though it contains no meat, this is actually a substantial dish with plenty of protein thanks to ingredients such as milk and eggs. You can serve this dish as an appetizer, a first course, or a side dish with boiled or grilled meat. This is a modern alternative to serving cardoons in the traditional way.

Prepare the stalks in the same way as in *Cardi al latte* (see page 186). Boil the cardoon stalks in abundant salty water for 30 minutes, until tender. Drain, then mince them. Preheat the oven to 350°F (180°C).

Prepare a béchamel sauce, put the butter and the flour in a saucepan over very low heat, whisking until they are completely blended. Meanwhile, put the milk in another saucepan over medium heat, and when it begins to rise, pour it, stirring continuously, into the saucepan where the butter and flour have been blended. Leave it on the fire at a very low flame, whisking continuously, for 1 to 2 minutes, until it is the consistency of yogurt, but not too thick. Remove the pan from the heat and stir in some salt and the grated Parmesan cheese.

Allow the mixture to cool to room temperature then stir in the egg yolks and the minced cardoon; taste and adjust for salt. Pour into a rectangular metal baking pan or a cupcake pan and bake for about 20 minutes.

If you have used a rectangular pan, cut even slices with a straight-edged spatula and remove them to serving plates. If you have used a cupcake mold, invert it over a platter or a tray so the individual soufflés drop out, then use your spatula to move them to serving plates. If you find you have a problem turning out this soufflé, next time bake it in an earthenware dish, bring it to the table, and serve it out with a spoon, thus finessing the problem. In any case, serve the soufflé immediately, dressed with grated Parmesan and black pepper.

Cavolfiore saltato
CAULIFLOWER WITH BUTTER AND PARMESAN
Serves 6

1 head cauliflower, trimmed
Salt
2½ tablespoons (35 g) unsalted butter
½ cup (65 g) grated Parmesan cheese, for serving
Freshly ground black pepper, for serving

This traditional recipe is very homely and simple, but it has the unquestionable advantage of being easily made in a short time. Serve it as a side dish with meat courses.

Put the cauliflower, abundant water, and a little salt in a pot with a lid, and bring to a boil over high heat. As soon as it comes to a boil, lower the heat just enough to still maintain the boil. Cook until the cauliflower is tender when prodded with a fork but still firm, 15 to 20 minutes. Drain, and sever the branches with a small, sharp knife; discard the stalk. Put the butter in a pan over very low heat. The butter should not sizzle, just melt. Stir the cauliflower into the melted butter and continue cooking over the low heat for about 5 minutes. Take off the stove and sprinkle—abundantly if you like—with grated Parmesan cheese and pepper.

Cavolfiore gratinato
CAULIFLOWER GRATIN
Serves 6

1 head cauliflower, trimmed
Salt
7 tablespoons (100 g) unsalted butter
2 tablespoons all-purpose (plain) flour
2 cups (500 ml) milk
⅓ teaspoon grated nutmeg
1½ cups (185 g) grated Parmesan cheese, plus ½ cup (65 g) for serving
Freshly ground black pepper, for serving

This, my own version, is a slightly more elaborate recipe than the last, although still a relatively simple one. You may cook a cauliflower specifically for this dish, or you can make this recipe using cauliflower boiled the previous day and now, cold and uninviting, unlikely to be eaten. Serve as a side dish.

Put the cauliflower, abundant water, and a little salt in a pot with a lid, and bring to a boil over high heat. Lower the heat just enough to maintain the boil. Cook until the stem is tender enough to pierce with a fork, but still firm, 15 to 20 minutes. Drain and, when it is cool enough to handle, cut it into small, even pieces (you may use the stalk, too).

Prepare a béchamel sauce with the butter, flour, milk, nutmeg, and 1½ cups Parmesan cheese as described in *Sformato di cardi* (see page 187).

Put the cauliflower pieces in an aluminum or ceramic baking pan and pour the béchamel sauce over them. Bake at 350°F (180°C) for 15 minutes. If your broiler is in the top of the oven, switch it on for the last few minutes to brown the upper crust a bit. Or, if

you aren't going to serve the dish immediately, take it out of the oven when it's cooked, and return it to the broiler to make the gratin crust just before bringing it to the table. Serve hot with the remaining Parmesan cheese and abundant pepper for those who may want it.

Cibreo
CHICKEN GIBLETS WITH FRESH HERBS, EGG, AND LEMON
Serves 6

4 chicken combs

8 chicken wattles

4 chicken hearts

4 chicken livers

3 to 4 tablespoons (50 to 60 ml) extra virgin olive oil

4 or 5 leaves sage

1 teaspoon chopped fresh rosemary

2 ounces (50 g) prosciutto, cut in thin cubes

1 clove garlic, peeled

¼ cup (60 ml) dry white wine

8 chicken kidneys

Salt

¼ cup (60 ml) meat stock (see page 24) or water, warmed

2 egg yolks

Juice of 1 lemon

Tuscan-style bread, for serving (see Choosing Ingredients)

Freshly ground black pepper, for serving

The chickens on the Calvelli farm have made a home under the rosemary bush.

According to the *Dictionary of the Accademia della Crusca*, the word *cibreo*, now identifying a specific dish, was in the past used as a synonym for "delicacy"—that is, good and skill-fully cooked food. Battaglia's etymologic dictionary suggests that the origin of the word *cibreo* is from an old definition of food for the gods—ambrosia. Through the years, the word has become less pompous and more familiar and intimate, so that it generally indicates good food, prepared to satisfy particular tastes and intended not merely for nourishment, but for enjoyment. "Do make a little *cibreo* for me" says Pinocchio, the puppet boy, during his orgy at the Red Shrimp Inn, where, among other delicacies, a partridge *cibreo* is served—thus it's not a specific recipe, but any particularly appetizing one.

I daresay that the application to a specific recipe, as we know it, derives from the fact that chicken giblets were considered privileged morsels, both for their taste and their protein content. If the chicken itself was eaten to appease the hunger of anyone at the table, the giblets were reserved for a specific diner who might need them for health reasons (such as a pregnant woman or a convalescent), or deserve them as a mark of privilege (for instance, the father of the family), or receive them simply out of the cook's love.

In Florence, few people nowadays use the word *cibreo* in the meaning of exquisite food. Anyone who still knows this word applies it to this dish, which is to be prepared with the special care devoted to preserving an endangered species. The quantity of chicken giblets given here is not enough for a main course, but the *cibreo* may be accompanied by a small *Sformato di spinaci* (see page 184) or served as an appetizer. If you have trouble finding the necessary chicken parts, try a Chinese market or ask a good butcher to order them for you.

In salted boiling water, blanch the combs and wattles for 10 minutes. Meanwhile, cut the hearts in half and check the livers for green smears of gall, discarding any that have them; otherwise, leave the livers whole. Drain the blanched wattles and combs, and cool them just enough so you can handle them. Skin the combs with a paring knife and cut them and the wattles into 2 or 3 pieces each. Put the hearts, combs, and wattles into a heavy cast-aluminum pan with the oil, sage, and rosemary over high heat, stirring and watching them constantly. When the giblets begin to brown, after about 5 minutes, add the livers, prosciutto, and garlic. Continue to brown, carefully turning the giblets. Be especially careful with the livers; turn them often with two spoons and avoid breaking them. About 5 minutes after you put in the livers, the browning will be nearly complete and the oil will begin to sizzle. Add the wine and kidneys, and a very little salt, stir gently, and scrape the sides to deglaze pan; leave on the stove another 2 to 3 minutes, allowing the wine to evaporate almost completely until you have a creamy sauce. Switch off the heat and cover the pan so that the liver finishes cooking with the residual heat. Taste and adjust the seasonings, if necessary.

When you are nearly ready to serve this dish, reheat it by pouring in the warm stock and turning the heat to very low for 2 minutes, stirring continuously. At this point the gravy should be creamy enough to serve the dish as it is.

While you are reheating the giblets, put the egg yolks and the lemon juice with a little salt in a bowl. Remove the giblet pan from the stove, and add the egg mixture. Stir with a wooden spoon for a few seconds, briskly enough so that it doesn't turn into an omelet, but gently enough so you don't break the livers. Serve with freshly baked bread and pepper for whoever likes it.

Crostini
CHICKEN LIVER TOASTS
Serves 8

⅓ cup (75 ml) extra virgin olive oil

1 red onion, minced

1 stalk celery, minced

1 carrot, peeled and minced

1 pound (500 g) chicken livers, coarsely chopped

3 salted anchovies, boned, rinsed, and coarsely chopped (see page 116)

4 tablespoons (100 g) capers, coarsely chopped

3 tablespoons (45 ml) Cognac

Salt

Up to ½ cup (125 ml) meat stock (see page 24) or water (optional)

7 tablespoons (100 g) unsalted butter

¾ pound (375 g) dense white bread

I use the name crostini without elaboration for this recipe, because for me the only crostini are those made with chicken liver. Nowadays there are many types in fashion—mostly undignified attempts to make appetizers of some sort—but once upon a time in Tuscany, any respectable celebration dinner was begun with chicken liver toasts dampened with meat stock. The tradition calls for the toasts to be wet, because generally, in a formal dinner, a stock-based first course follows after the appetizer, thus the stock is ready at hand. I will give you this method and a dry alternative—try both ways to test the difference and decide which you prefer. Serve crostini as an appetizer.

First, prepare the soffritto. Heat the oil over medium heat. Add the onion, celery, and carrot and sauté, stirring often and watching constantly, until the soffritto is a nice golden brown, about 10 minutes. At this point, add the livers, anchovies, and capers. Mix well, and add the Cognac and only a little salt (because of the presence of the anchovies). Cook for about 10 minutes until the livers are pink inside, but have no trace of blood. If you need more liquid to complete cooking, it would be best to use stock.

Remove the pan from the stove and purée the contents, still hot, in a food mill, a food processor, or a blender. If you use a food mill, you may want to beat the purée with an electric mixer at high speed to obtain a smooth, elegant texture. Mix in the butter, which should melt into the mixture if it has not cooled too much.

To make the traditional, wet crostini, cut the bread into rounds about ½ inch (1 cm) thick with or without the crusts, of whatever size you wish. Toast the rounds well, so that they are completely dry both outside and inside. Otherwise, when the stock is poured on, the toasts will collapse. To serve, put a generous tablespoon of the liver purée on each toast round. Place the crostini on a serving platter. Pour on a ladleful of warm stock just before serving. If you prefer, you may omit the stock and serve the crostini dry.

Fegato alla veneziana
CALF'S LIVER VENETIAN STYLE
Serves 6

4 large white onions, thinly sliced
½ cup (125 ml) extra virgin olive oil
2 or 3 fresh or canned tomatoes, peeled
Salt
6 slices calf's liver (about 1 pound or 500 g total)
Freshly ground black pepper, for serving

Fegato alla veneziana is a classic and rather popular Italian recipe. I also give you a variation, different mostly as to procedure, which is devised to make this dish not better (because it is already good enough) but more "sparkling." I cannot find a more suitable word for it. This main course does not require any side dish because it includes vegetables.

Put the onions and the oil in a pan over medium heat until they soften and reduce in volume, about 15 minutes. If the onions become dry before they are soft and beginning to caramelize, add some water, one ladle at a time. When the onions are properly browned, add the tomatoes, squashing them with a fork, and a pinch of salt. Continue cooking for another 10 minutes. Now add the liver slices to the pan, cover them with the onions and tomatoes, and cook for 2 minutes on each side. If you will not serve the dish right away, wait until the last minute to cook the liver; otherwise the liver will harden when reheated. To reheat,

A produce vendor shows off his grand display of tomatoes near Sant'Ambrogio market.

warm the onions in the pan and add the liver. Serve hot, one slice and a portion of the onions for each person; put pepper on the table for whoever likes it.

VARIATION WITH ONION, SAGE, AND GARLIC MIXTURE

3 tablespoons (50 ml) extra virgin olive oil
6 to 8 leaves sage
1 clove garlic, sliced

This second version of my own is similar, except for a few details. When the onion is duly browned, squash 1 or 2 tomatoes in the pan and keep cooking for 2 to 3 minutes more, then switch the flame off and leave to rest. When mealtime arrives, reheat the onions, and, in another pan, fry the liver slices with the oil, sage, and garlic, 2 minutes on each side. This should be done over a high flame, so that the liver surface is slightly crunchy on both sides of the slice. Serve hot, covering each liver slice with the hot onion mixture.

The main difference in the second version is that the liver and the onions are not stewed together, and the liver slices are a bit crunchy outside. The combination of tastes, instead of being made by the stewing together of the components, is made directly in the mouth. This may seem a minor thing, but the difference in taste is remarkable.

◆

Benedetta playing in the surf on the shore of the Tyrrhenian Sea.

Baccalà alla livornese
SALT COD LIVORNO STYLE
Serves 6

2⅔ pounds (1½ kg) baccalà (salt cod fillets), reconstituted, cut in 6 pieces

½ cup (70 g) all-purpose (plain) flour

½ to 1 cup (125 to 250 ml) extra virgin olive oil, for frying, plus 4 tablespoons (60 ml) for the sauce

3 cloves garlic, minced

½ cup (30 g) minced flat-leaf parsley

2 teaspoons ground chile pepper (see Choosing Ingredients)

2 pounds (1 kg) canned peeled tomatoes, drained

Salt

There are various types of *baccalà* (salt cod), and it is more and more difficult to find the best ones. The same fish, when dried, is called stockfish, and is now rarely available except in regions such as Liguria where it is part of the local tradition. For both salt cod and stockfish, the operations necessary to make them edible—desalinization and rehydration—are so time-consuming that very few shops still do it. Look for it in fish markets and in the seafood section of good supermarkets. Choose reconstituted salt cod that comes in the largest fillets possible. Here I give you two versions of the dish, the first the traditional one and the second, a little lighter. Whichever way you choose to make it, serve this dish as a main course.

Dredge each piece of cod in the flour and set aside. Put enough oil to cover just over half the depth of the fillets in a frying pan over high heat. Test the heat of the oil in the usual way by tossing in a bread crumb, when it sizzles it is ready. Put the cod pieces in the oil all at once if the pieces will fit; otherwise, cook them in batches. Fry for about 3 minutes per side, until they are a light golden color. Transfer them to absorbent paper. Avoid stacking the slices; they will drain better in a single layer.

Separately, prepare the sauce. Combine the garlic, parsley, chile, and the 4 tablespoons of oil in a baking pan big enough to accommodate all the pieces of cod. (I use rectangular oven trays for *baccalà* because the rectangular fish pieces fit better into them.) Open the cans of peeled tomatoes and set them beside the stove, because you must be quick in adding them. Set the baking pan on the stove over medium heat until the oil begins to sizzle. Stir continuously while the oil heats: Do not allow the garlic to burn (you will notice the stink if garlic starts to burn). Add the tomatoes as soon as you hear the oil sizzling, squashing them in the pan with a fork, and add a very little salt. Cook for about 5 minutes, then add the salt cod to the sauce and cook for another 2 minutes on each side. Serve hot.

Practically everything is the same in the second version, except that the cod is not fried. Instead, flour the pieces and immerse them in the sauce exactly as you did in the first recipe, but cook them a little longer, about 3 minutes on a side.

Either version of this dish can be prepared in advance—this would not spoil them at all. To reheat, observe these rules: If the cod is fried, switch off the fire when you immerse the pieces into the sauce (rather than cooking them for the additional 2 minutes per side) and, when you're ready to serve the dish, cover the pan with aluminum foil and reheat in a 300°F (150°C) oven for about 10 minutes. If the fish is not fried, cook it first for a shorter time (3 or 4 minutes as opposed to 6) and reheat it in the oven as above.

Baccalà mantecato
SALT COD IN MILK SAUCE
Serves 6

1¾ pounds (800 g) baccalà (salt cod fillets), reconstituted (see page 197)
1 carrot, peeled and cut in large pieces
1 stalk celery, cut in large pieces
1 red onion, cut in large pieces
1 cup (250 ml) milk
1 cup (250 ml) extra virgin olive oil
Freshly ground black pepper
White bread croutons or fried polenta, for serving

This dish is traditional of the Veneto region, and I like it—really love it, in fact. You can find it, done quite well, in top restaurants, but also at the *bacari,* nice small inns where one generally goes for a drink. At these places the *ombra* (small glasses) of wine are accompanied by snacks, among which *baccalà mantecato* on toast is the most characteristic. If you are not under twenty years old—if you are, you probably don't really know what wine is—and if you happen to be in Venice, I heartily suggest that you make the *bacari* run. To find them you should watch for a couple of old Venetian men and follow them around. Probably you won't make it to the end of their run, but try anyway. It's better to attempt it in the morning lest you spoil your tourist's schedule, because after returning to the hotel you will feel the compelling need for a good nap. As the Latin proverb goes, *semel in anno licet insanire*: It is permitted to do crazy things, but only once a year.

Once I was extravagant in complimenting the cook of a Venetian restaurant who made an excellent version of this dish, much better than my own! I obtained, in exchange, the revelation of a secret that was indeed essential, and in my turn, and without requiring compliments, I hand it down to you. My mistake had been that, in addition to the bones, I also removed the skin of the cod, which is essential for giving a creamy texture to the milk sauce. Enjoy this wonderful dish and kiss the calorie count goodbye! In Venice, this dish is served as a main course, but I prefer to use it as an appetizer.

See *Baccalà alla livornese* (page 197) for advice on choosing the salt cod. Put enough cold water to cover the fish in a pot with the fish, carrot, celery, and onion, and bring it to a boil over medium heat. As soon as the water boils, remove from the heat and let the pot stand for 5 minutes, then remove the fish with a skimmer and lay it on absorbent paper to drain and cool. When the *baccalà* is cool enough to handle, remove all the bones, a necessarily manual operation. Do not remove the skin, however.

◆

Tuscan men find good conversation in the Piazza della Repubblica.

Put the milk in a pan over low heat, and heat it until it is hot, taking care not to boil or burn it. Meanwhile, crumble the *baccalà* by hand and put it in a bowl. Use a pestle to pulverize the fish, stopping every now and then to whisk in, alternately, trickles of oil and hot milk. Go back and forth between using the pestle and whisk. Continue to beat tirelessly; the process should take about 15 minutes. Salt is not normally necessary, but do add some black pepper. If the mixture gets too cold to mix well during the mashing, reheat it in a bain-marie until it is sufficiently malleable. You should also reheat it until it's warm when you are about to serve it. Accompany it with croutons of white bread or fried polenta.

Crocchette di baccalà
CODFISH CROQUETTES
Serves 6

1¼ pounds (800 g) baccalà (salt cod fillets), reconstituted
7 tablespoons (100 g) unsalted butter
3 tablespoons all-purpose (plain) flour, plus more for coating
2 cups (500 ml) milk
Salt
Pinch of grated nutmeg
2 eggs
Freshly ground black pepper
Extra virgin olive oil, for frying

This is a dish from my childhood, which recalls a lot of memories. Don't ask if it is good; I like it very much. Serve as a main course with a radicchio salad.

Boil the salt cod as in *Baccalà mantecato* (see page 198). When the fish is cool enough to handle, remove the bones and skin with your fingers, and mince the fish with a knife as finely as you can.

Prepare a béchamel sauce with the butter, flour, milk, and a little salt (see page 188), but leave it on the fire at a very low flame, whisking often, for about 3 to 4 minutes or until it is the consistency of porridge or oatmeal. Sprinkle the nutmeg on the sauce and mix in the cod, eggs, and a bit of pepper until the mixture is thick enough to form into balls that will hold their shape. Form the mixture between your palms into croquettes about the size of ping-pong balls (or in any case smaller than an egg) and in whatever shape you like. Set them on a plate and dust them with flour.

Fry the croquettes in oil deep enough to half cover them for 4 to 5 minutes, turning them once, until they are a deep golden color, crispy outside yet soft and moist inside. If you need a reminder of frying techniques, see *Crocchette* (page 114). Croquettes tend to break up when turned. To avoid this, grasp them lightly between two spoons or forks and turn them with a single, quick motion. When they are done, remove them from the oil with a slotted spoon and lay them on absorbent paper. Serve hot.

◆

Benedetta and Cristina inspect a porcini mushroom in the Zibibbo kitchen.

Alchemy
in the
Kitchen

alchemy in the kitchen

The last topic of this book is a difficult one for me: I may risk being taken for a lunatic in talking about it. The word *alchemy* in the title of this chapter is used in the meaning of "transformation"—and, indeed, to me cooking involves transforming foods for the better. Though the word may be used without hinting at the magic still associated with it, I am nevertheless attracted by the element of mystery in this transformation process. Inventiveness, love, and personal involvement are necessary ingredients in any recipe, to which magic may rightfully be added QB—*quanto basta,* just the right amount—as any respectable Italian cookbook would do. A little magic helps transform shapeless and unordered matter, not into gold or the elixir of life perhaps, but into a unique compound, balanced and beneficial to humankind.

History has recognized the origin of alchemy in the craftsman's procedures for transforming metals, initially a jealously kept secret asset of the priestly caste of Alexandrine Egypt. Their theories and techniques, cloaked in a mantle of sacredness and mystery, spawned a complex and fascinating system of symbols, handed down through the centuries until the advent of modern science. The alchemist's search for a unique balance left each single piece of laboriously gleaned knowledge without value unless it could fit into a universal system. Nowadays such thinking is far from our modern approach to knowledge, which sorts the wide-ranging responsibilities of the alchemist into various fields of research.

In times long past, a little mystery was boiling in the kettles, and not only in the witch's cauldron or in the alchemist's still. Today very little survives of the ancient mystery; even the so-called cook's secrets have all but disappeared. Nevertheless, we like to think that cooking is not merely mincing, cutting, skinning, and so on, but it is also a way to express ourselves, thus mixing a bit of ourselves into the recipe. The best cooking reflects the cook's personal influence, an additional ingredient in a dish we used to call "hand." The phrase "that chef is a great hand" means not only that he has mastered the techniques or that he is knowledgeable, but also that he adds something more. It may not be necessary or even possible to identify that thing, but there is a subtle difference in these cooks' creations, untraceable if you look only to the mechanical procedures for preparing a dish.

♦

Prepared meat is rolled and bound tightly between two sticks to keep air from entering and spoiling it. (above)

♦

A pastry chef puts an artful twist in a brioche. (left)

Cipolle al forno
WEARY ONIONS
Serves 6

6 red onions, peeled and halved crosswise

Salt

Freshly ground black pepper

1 tablespoon chopped fresh oregano, or 1 teaspoon dried

1 cup (250 ml) extra virgin olive oil

1 cup (250 ml) dry red wine

1 to 2 cups (250 to 500 ml) meat stock (see page 24), water, or red wine (optional)

Tuscan-style bread, for serving (see Choosing Ingredients)

This dish is not particularly difficult to prepare, but it requires great attention, especially in the cooking. This operation would ideally require a wood oven, or at least a good ordinary oven with steam injection. The onion quality is important. They should be red, not very dry, sugary, and of medium size. If you are able to find the type called Tropea, after the town near Naples where they are grown, they are the best. This dish can be served as a first course, as a side dish with every kind of meat, or however you like, hot or cold.

Cut the bottom off each onion half to make a base, and set them upright in a baking pan. Sprinkle them with some salt and pepper and the oregano, and pour the oil and wine over them.

So far so good, and simple. The tricky part arises with baking. The aim is to have well-cooked onions, soft enough to melt in the mouth, but they should also taste totally different from boiled or stewed onions. The dish must taste of baked onions and, to that end, two or sometimes even three stages of baking are required. Put the pan in the oven heated to 400°F (250°C), and brown the onions for 30 minutes. Then reduce the heat to 250°F (125°C) and bake for 30 minutes or so, using steam set at half the full setting if you are lucky enough to have a baker's oven with a steam-injection system, or else covering the baking dish tightly with aluminum foil to keep the moisture in. During the baking, test the onions with a fork. When they are fully soft, they are ready. At the end of baking, 10 minutes of high heat 400°F (250°C) may again be required, both to give a good final browning of the onions and to condense somewhat the juices formed during baking. Throughout the time the onions are in the oven, you should frequently check the level of

A basket full of red onions sits amongst rows of black cabbage and fennel.

liquid, which must never dry out completely. If necessary, pour in some stock, water, or red wine. The name of the recipe suggests the look of the onions at the end of baking. In addition to being much reduced in volume, they should be squat and soft and look as if they are very tired.

Let the dish rest for about 15 minutes before serving with abundant fresh white bread to soak up the cooking juice, formed by the oil, wine, and onion juices.

Peperoni al forno
BAKED YELLOW SWEET PEPPERS
Serves 6

3 yellow bell peppers (capsicums), halved and seeded
12 Greek-style black olives, pitted
1 tablespoon capers, drained
6 salted anchovies, boned, rinsed, and cut in 2 to 3 pieces (see page 116)
1 fresh or canned tomato, peeled and sliced
1 tablespoon chopped fresh oregano
½ cup (125 ml) extra virgin olive oil, plus 2 tablespoons (30 ml)
Salt
Freshly ground black pepper
½ cup (125 ml) dry red wine, plus 2 tablespoons (30 ml)
½ cup meat stock (see page 24), or water (optional)

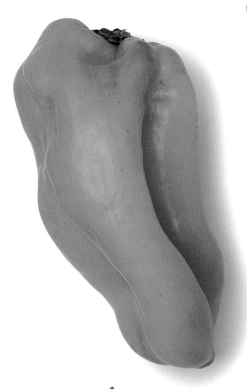

Sweet yellow pepper

This dish can be served as an appetizer or as a side dish to a main course. Fill each pepper half with 2 olives, a few capers, 2 or 3 pieces of anchovy, a slice of tomato, some oregano, a teaspoon (5 ml) of oil, salt, pepper, and a teaspoon (5 ml) of red wine. Put the pepper halves in a baking pan surrounded by the remaining ½ cup of oil and ½ cup of red wine.

Baking of this type is much easier in steam-injection ovens especially when dealing with vegetables such as onions and sweet peppers that require long baking times. If you don't have a steam-injection oven, cover the dish with aluminum foil and bake for 20 minutes at 175°F (140°C). If you do have a steam-injection oven, do not cover the dish but program it so steam is released. When the peppers are tender and a concentrated sauce has formed, uncover the pan (or discontinue the steam), and continue baking for 10 minutes more. When they are done, the peppers will be very soft and will be surrounded by a liquid made up of the evaporated wine, oil, and the other ingredients' juices. Make sure to check, especially in the final stage, that some liquid always remains. If necessary, pour in some stock or water. Transfer to a serving plate and serve hot, warm, or even cold.

Cozze ripiene
STUFFED MUSSELS
Serves 6

2 pounds (1 kg) mussels, scrubbed and debearded

¼ cup (60 ml) dry white wine

3 cloves garlic, minced

1 bunch flat-leaf parsley, minced

1 cup (100 g) dried bread crumbs

1 egg

½ cup (65 g) grated Parmesan cheese

1 teaspoon ground chile pepper (see Choosing Ingredients)

¼ cup (60 ml) extra virgin olive oil

1 pound (500 g) fresh or canned tomatoes, peeled

This is a great dish, seldom served, and uncommon even in good seafood restaurants. The recipe is not difficult, but it has the drawback of requiring that the mussels be tied one by one. It is best to use fairly large mussels for this dish. Serve as a main course with a salad of green radicchio or romaine lettuce.

Put the mussels in a large pot with the wine; cover tightly with a lid, and place over high heat. Cook for about 5 minutes, until the mussels have all opened. Take the mussels out of the pot, discarding any that haven't opened, and reserving the cooking liquid. When they are cool enough to handle, take the mussels out of their shells without separating the two halves of the shell. Set the shells aside. Mince the mussels on a chopping board. Pour the cooking liquid through a cloth napkin or clean kitchen towel to filter out any solids.

To make the filling, combine all but 1 tablespoon of the garlic and 2 tablespoons of the parsley, with the minced mussel flesh in a bowl with the bread crumbs, egg, and Parmesan cheese, and mix well. If the mixture is too dry and will not stick together, add part of the filtered mussel cooking liquid and mix well until it can be formed into balls. Fill the mussel shells one by one and close them, tying the valves together with pieces of kitchen string.

Prepare a Livornese sauce: combine the remaining 1 tablespoon garlic, 2 tablespoons parsley, the chile pepper, and the oil in a pan over medium heat, stirring so the garlic doesn't burn. As soon as the oil begins to sizzle, add the tomatoes, squashing them with a fork, then add ⅓ cup (75 ml) of the filtered mussel cooking liquid. Cook, stirring, for 5 minutes, then add the mussels and continue cooking for 10 minutes, turning the mussels over once halfway through. Turn off the heat and remove the tied-up mussels from the sauce with a slotted spoon. Let them sit until they are cool enough to handle, then remove the strings and put the mussels back in the sauce. Reheat gently before serving. Spoon equal amounts of mussels and sauce into 6 serving dishes, or, if you prefer, remove and throw away the upper (empty) shells, set the filled shells on serving plates, and distribute the sauce on top of each mussel.

Pesciolini in scapeccio
FRIED WHITEBAIT
Serves 6

½ cup (125 ml) extra virgin olive oil, plus 2 tablespoons (30 ml) for serving
1¾ pounds (800 g) whitebait
½ yellow onion, sliced in thin strips
2 cloves garlic, chopped
1 bunch flat-leaf parsley, chopped
⅓ cup (75 ml) white wine vinegar
Salt
1 fresh chile pepper, minced, or a pinch of ground chile pepper (optional) (see Choosing Ingredients)

Scapeccio, scapece, or similar terms depending on regional variations, is a cooking method enabling the cooked food—generally vegetables or fish—to be preserved for a limited period of time. The technique is to fry the food first and then put it in vinegar and oil, finishing with herbs and other flavoring ingredients according to the various

At Lake Massaciúccoli,
*people living along the canals
use dip nets to catch eel
and other fish.*

A variety of fish ready for auction at the Viareggio wholesale market.

recipes. The young of various small fish such as herring—the small fry called white-bait—are called *zeri* (zeros) in Italian. These are fish so small they can be fried and eaten whole, like chips. All operations described in this recipe should be done with the utmost care, because these fish are very fragile, especially when cooked. Serve as an appetizer, or as a main course with tomato and basil salad.

Choose a frying pan wide enough to accommodate all the fish at once, and pour in the ½ cup (125 ml) of oil. Heat the oil over high until it comes to a gentle boil. When the oil is hot enough, put the whitebait in the pan and fry them until they begin to crackle, about 5 minutes. Retrieve the fish from the oil with a skimmer or slotted spoon and drain them thoroughly on absorbent paper. Place them on a wide platter with high sides and scatter around the onion strips, a little of the garlic and parsley, the vinegar, and the remaining oil. Add salt judiciously and, if you like, a little chile pepper. I have given you quantities to go by, but keep in mind that these are dressings, so judge for yourself. Tasting is essential.

This dish must rest for at least 20 to 30 minutes in order to absorb the vinegar. You may prepare it in the morning for dinner, but it may also be preserved in the refrigerator, well-wrapped, for no more than 2 days; after that it becomes too sharp.

Passato di pesce
TUSCAN FISH PURÉE
Serves 8

½ cup (125 ml) extra virgin olive oil

2 red onions, 1 minced and 1 coarsely chopped

2 carrots, peeled, 1 minced and 1 coarsely chopped

2 stalks celery, 1 minced and 1 coarsely chopped

2 fresh or canned tomatoes, peeled

2½ pounds (1¼ kg) potatoes, peeled and cubed

1 pound (500 g) whole cleaned fish with heads on,
   such as scorpion fish, red mullet, cod, rockfish, or shelled and deveined shrimp (prawns)

5 cloves garlic, 3 minced and 2 whole

1 fresh chile pepper, minced, or a pinch of ground chile pepper (optional) (see Choosing Ingredients)

Salt

Tuscan-style bread, for serving (see Choosing Ingredients)

There are countless varieties of puréed fish soups in Italy, from region to region and from coast to coast. Next, I'll give you the one that is the most popular in Tuscany, and which I prefer—not because I want to start a parochial dispute, but for no other reason than its red color, which I think makes it better looking than the various *brodetti* (strained fish soups), which look somehow grayish.

The choice of fish is paramount. One to be considered is the *scorfano* (Mediterranean stonefish or scorpion fish, the *rascasse* of bouillabaisse), which is a very tasty reef dweller. Or you may use red mullet. Various types of fish can be used, keeping in mind that those with white and delicate flesh give a daintier taste, but in this type of soup it is appropriate to balance the delicate with something strong and sharp. In any case, bluefish or clupeids (sardines, mackerel, herring, tuna, and the like) are not to be used, while a few shrimp would be acceptable, as long as you add them at the end of cooking (because they cook in very few minutes). This is a first course.

Start by making a soffritto. In a metal pot large enough to contain the whole soup, heat the oil over a medium flame. Add the minced onion, minced carrot, and minced celery and sauté, stirring often and watching constantly, until the soffritto is a light golden color, about 10 minutes. When the soffritto is done, add the tomatoes, squashing them with a fork and cooking them with the soffritto for a couple of minutes. Add the chopped onion, carrot, and celery, the potatoes, the fish, half of the minced garlic, and as much chile pepper as you like (fish purées are better if a little spicy), then cover with water by 1 inch (2 cm). Be very conservative when adding salt.

Simmer, uncovered for about 20 minutes. When the carrot is cooked, everything else will be, too. Retrieve the largest fish and remove their bones but leave their heads attached. Return the fish to the soup and strain everything through a food mill (sorry, no alternative) at least twice. Add the remaining minced garlic and check for salt. Serve with sliced bread, toasted on both sides and rubbed with the garlic cloves. Don't pour the purée on top of the bread, as it shouldn't soak in, but dish up the purée first and place the toasted bread on top.

Mamme ripiene

STUFFED GIANT ARTICHOKES

Serves 5

10 very large, tender artichokes

Salt

7 ounces (200 g) good-quality beef, minced

3 eggs

⅔ cup (85 g) grated Parmesan cheese

Pinch of grated nutmeg

Freshly ground black pepper

1 cup (100 g) cubed Tuscan-style bread (see Choosing Ingredients)

1 cup (250 ml) milk

1 cup (100 g) dried bread crumbs

1 to 2 cups (250 to 500 ml) extra virgin olive oil

½ cup (125 ml) meat stock (see page 24) or water

Artichokes that grow one on each plant, on top of its main stalk, which are much larger than the usual ones and have a bulging base—we call these artichokes *mamme* (mothers). They are available in May and June. This main course requires no side dish.

Pull off all the hard outer leaves—all of them, I repeat, because it is very disturbing to put in the mouth a thing which can in no way be chewed! With a paring knife trim off the top third of the remaining leaves. Cut off the stalk and the bottom of the artichoke, to make a flat base. With your fingers, spread open the center leaves, insert your paring knife, and cut out the choke. Put enough salted water to cover the artichokes in a large pot. Bring to a boil, and place the artichokes in the pot. Blanch for no more than 5 minutes, just enough to start cooking. Retrieve the artichokes with a skimmer, taking care not to break them, and set them aside to drain on a clean surface.

In a bowl, combine the beef, 1 egg, the Parmesan cheese, nutmeg, and some salt and pepper. Separately, soak the cubed bread in the milk for 5 minutes, then retrieve the bread and add it to the beef and egg mixture. Mix well with your hands. If the resulting mixture is too dry to stick together, use some of the milk in which you soaked the bread to moisten it a little.

Take 1 artichoke at a time and very gently open the inner leaves outward, and place 2 heaping tablespoons (about 40 ml) of filling in the center, filling from the top. Flatten

*A newborn lamb rests
under the careful watch of its mother.*

the upper surface of the filling with the palm of your hand. When all the artichokes are stuffed, beat together the remaining 2 eggs in a bowl with a pinch of salt. Put the bread crumbs in another bowl. In a frying pan over high heat, heat enough oil to come ½ inch (1½ cm) up the side of the pan. When the oil is sizzling, very quickly, dunk the top of an artichoke (where the filling shows) first in the egg, then in the crumbs, and set the artichoke upside-down in the pan, so that the stuffed and coated side is in the oil. Fry the artichokes for 3 minutes in batches if necessary, and when each is done, set it upright (on its stem end) in a baking dish with ¼ cup (60 ml) oil and ½ cup meat stock. Bake the artichokes for about 20 minutes at 300°F (150°C), until tender. Serve hot, but if the dish rests a little it will not suffer; simply reheat it in the oven at a moderate temperature, about 240°F (120°C), just before serving.

Agnello in fricassea
LAMB WITH EGG-LEMON SAUCE
Serves 4

½ cup (125 ml) extra virgin olive oil
2 pounds (1 kg) lamb shoulder, cut in 1-inch (2-cm) cubes
3 or 4 leaves sage
Leaves from 1 sprig of rosemary
2 cloves garlic, coarsely chopped
½ cup (125 ml) dry white wine
Salt
2 cups (500 ml) water
2 egg yolks
Juice of 2 lemons
Freshly ground black pepper, for serving

In this recipe the base ingredient is lamb, but it could be rabbit, chicken, chunks of veal, or even boiled beef. Serve as a main course accompanied by sautéed artichokes or asparagus.

Choose a fairly wide, heavy cast-aluminum pot that can accommodate all the meat in a single layer. Heat the oil over medium heat until it begins to bubble, and add the lamb. Brown for about 20 minutes, turning the pieces so they brown on all sides. When the browning is nearly complete, add the sage, rosemary, and garlic. Keep stirring, taking care that the garlic doesn't burn. Pour in the wine, turn the heat to high, and let the wine evaporate almost completely. Add some salt and the water, reduce the heat to low, cover, and cook for another 45 minutes. Frequently check the level of the liquid and stir with a wooden spoon, adding more hot water only as necessary so the lamb does not dry out. Toward the end of the cooking, check the lamb with a fork; it should be tender. The juice that remains should not be liquid, but thick.

Right before you are ready to serve the lamb, gently combine the egg yolks and lemon juice in a bowl. Take the pot with the lamb off the stove and stirring continuously with a wooden spoon, pour in the egg and lemon. Keep stirring until a smooth, creamy sauce has formed. If you do not keep stirring, or if you leave the pot on the stove, you will have an omelet.

After you add the egg and lemon, the lamb cannot be reheated, so finish the *fricassea* at the very moment before serving. Serve hot, with pepper at the table.

Stracotto al latte
VEAL STEWED WITH MILK
Serves 6

½ cup (125 ml) extra virgin olive oil

2 pounds (1 kg) girello (veal top round), in one piece

2 or 3 leaves sage

2 teaspoons chopped fresh rosemary

2 cloves garlic, sliced

2 cups (500 ml) milk

¾ cup (175 ml) dry red wine

1 large red onion, finely chopped

1 carrot, peeled and finely chopped

1 stalk celery, finely chopped

Salt

Meat stock (see page 24), or water (optional)

1 tablespoon (15 ml) prepared mustard

Stracotto, meaning "overcooked," indicates a stew made with a whole joint of meat. The following recipe should be followed carefully, step by step, because the details are very important for an excellent result. It will be edible in any case, but let us not settle for the mediocre. This is a main course, and it can be accompanied by *Puré di patate* (see page 31) or cardoons.

Put the oil in a large metal pan over high heat until it starts to sizzle. Put the meat, sage, and rosemary in the oil and brown for 15 minutes, turning the meat regularly so that all sides obtain an even browning. Just before the browning is complete, add the garlic. When the meat is well browned, add the milk, wine, onion, carrot, celery, and a little salt. Turn the heat down to low to maintain a simmer, and cover. Cook for about 1½ hours. As the level of liquid decreases, part of the meat will remain uncovered, so turn it often and check that it does not dry out. Maintain 1 inch (2 to 3 cm) of liquid in the bottom of the pan. Check the liquid level from time to time, and add hot stock as necessary.

When the veal is tender, take it out of the pan and set it on a cutting board or platter to rest. Turn the heat up to high to condense the sauce, stirring constantly with a wooden spoon for 5 to 7 minutes. Pay close attention: When the milk, previously congealed turns creamy, remove the pan from the stove. Put the cooked vegetables through a food mill into a bowl. Stir in the mustard to complete the sauce. Cut the meat in slices about ¼ inch (½ cm) thick, and reassemble the joint in a container where it fits rather tightly, alternating meat slices and sauce, and pouring all the remaining sauce on top. Leave for a few hours in the refrigerator to allow the flavors to combine. When ready to serve, transfer the veal slices and sauce from the container to the top bowl of a bain-marie (see page 135) or double boiler to reheat. When hot, place the veal in a serving bowl or serve directly onto plates, covering each slice with a ladle of sauce.

Sage

Torta di fichi

FRESH FIG TORTE

Serves 6

7 tablespoons (100 g) unsalted butter, at room temperature

½ cup (70 g) all-purpose (plain) flour

4 egg yolks

1¼ cups (350 g) sugar

1¼ cups (300 ml) milk

3 tablespoons (50 ml) blackberry jam

20 very ripe figs, quartered

◆

Torta di fichi

At the end of every memorable meal a special dessert is required. Here is one we serve at Zibibbo when figs are ripe in Florence. In Tuscany, the best figs are called *verdini;* they're intensely dark red inside a green skin.

Prepare a pastry dough of the kind we call a *pasta frolla* (*frolla* means crumbly): In a mixing bowl, combine the butter, flour, 1 egg yolk, and ¼ cup (50 g) of the sugar. Knead it with your hands just long enough to make the ingredients stick together. Cover with plastic wrap, and allow the dough to rest in the refrigerator for ½ hour.

Preheat the oven to 350°F (180°C). Roll the dough directly over the bottom and ½ inch (1 cm) up the sides of a spring-form pie or torte pan with a diameter of 11 to 12 inches (28 to 30 cm). You can also roll out the dough on a piece of marble or any smooth surface and transfer it to the pan. It's better not to add any flour while rolling. Bake for approximately 15 minutes, until it turns a beautiful golden brown color. Take the baked shell out of the pan and place it on a serving platter.

While the torte shell is baking, make the pastry cream. In a bowl, energetically whisk the remaining 3 egg yolks with the remaining 1½ cups (300 g) sugar until it changes color from yellow to nearly white, 3 to 4 minutes. In a saucepan over low heat, warm the milk until it begins to bubble and rise up, then remove it from the stove and stir in the egg mixture with a wooden spoon. Put the pan back on the stove over low heat, stirring constantly for 1 to 2 minutes, until it thickens a little, then remove from the heat and stir the jam quickly into the hot milk with a whisk or wooden spoon. Spread this mixture on the baked torte shell, and set the fig quarters in concentric circles on top of the torte. Allow to cool to room temperature before serving. Leftovers can be kept in the refrigerator until the next day.

Afterword

afterword

When our efforts in the kitchen don't turn out the way we expected, it is not just that "that's the way the cookie crumbles." There are many reasons why things might have gone awry: The ingredients are not right, or they are cooked for the wrong length of time, in the wrong pots, with insufficient attention due to overconfidence or distraction, or just because we're in a bad mood. It's not the end of the world. It happens to the best of us.

Sometimes we must simply try and try again, keeping at it until we achieve the desired results. It seems to me that in this respect cooking is no different from any other human activity.

We must keep trying because good cooking is a pleasure we should not forego.

We must keep trying because, no matter what the style of cooking—be it vegetarian, Ayurvedic, weight-reducing, French, Italian, or Senegalese—whether the recipe is good or bad, our discerning choice of ingredients and the care we put into preparation will always create something of value, ephemeral but precious.

We must keep trying because our connection with nature grows ever more attenuated, more distant and distracted. We are so preoccupied with our daily business that we forget we are part of nature ourselves, and we deny ourselves the enjoyment of living fully.

We must keep trying because the acts of choosing ingredients, discovering new products and new recipes, cooking, and eating with pleasure all bring us together and help keep us together.

We must keep trying because if we do not, we condemn ourselves to a future of energy bars, mad cows, and mercury-laden fish.

We must keep trying because if we do not we will suffer from sadness, in addition to all the other pathologies caused by bad food.

It seems to me that we absolutely must keep trying, for why else have I written this book?

We must keep trying
because good cooking
is a pleasure
we should not forego.

A cypress-lined alley leads to a villa in San Casciano Val de Pesa.

choosing ingredients

Most Tuscan dishes do not involve elaborate procedures or expensive ingredients. What they do require is careful attention to the choice of ingredients and to their preparation. Most of our ingredients are fairly common and can be found anywhere. Often organically grown produce has the most flavor.

It is a universal axiom of good cooking that the fresher the vegetables, herbs, fruit, meat, and fish, the better. I happen to live next door to one of the best market squares in Florence. I am there at 7:00 every morning but Sunday. Across the street from my restaurant is a small farm that supplies me with freshly picked vegetables and where my cooks can cut herbs as they need them.

In Italy, as in all modern countries, many kinds of vegetables and fruits are available all year round, being grown in greenhouses or imported from other places. But to me, there is no point in using these things, because the local produce that is in season is so much better. We adjust our menu almost every day according to what is available and good. Some of my favorite foods have very limited seasons, such as *agretti*, a green vegetable that only appears in March and that I have never seen elsewhere, and *bacelli*, fresh green fava beans that come in April and are eaten raw with pecorino cheese.

Some foods we use either fresh or not, depending on the season. Tomatoes for sauces, for example, may be either fresh or canned. Oregano and marjoram are very nice when they are fresh, but they are fine dried, too.

I am often asked about substituting for ingredients that are out of season or hard to find. When it is possible to substitute for something in a recipe, I give the other possibilities. But in many dishes there is simply no substitute for the key ingredients. There are many traditional Tuscan dishes for which I have not given recipes in this book because I believe the reader's chances of finding the ingredients outside of our region are too slim. In a few cases, though, I give recipes that call for such ingredients because they are good examples of what Tuscan cooking is all about. If these recipes interest you, perhaps you will consider it worth your time to seek out the ingredients.

Here are some descriptions to help you find and choose appropriate ingredients for Tuscan dishes.

◆

Freshly picked peaches from the Calvelli farm are ready for market. (above)

◆

Benedetta shops the market with all her senses. (left)

Paulo Salvini with a bucket
of freshly picked cardoons
from his market garden in the
Careggi district of Florence.

ANCHOVIES

These small fish used to be caught in the Mediterranean Sea in large quantities before many of the best fishing grounds became too polluted. In Tuscany, we still use them fresh, from the fishmonger, but more often dried and salted, sold from barrels. The salted ones must be rinsed thoroughly under running water and their bones removed with the fingers. Outside of the Mediterranean countries, anchovies are now most commonly sold as fillets packed in oil. These are to be avoided if at all possible. It is better to use canned salted fillets that can be found in Italian grocery stores marked *filetti d'acciuga* or *acciughe sotto sale*.

ARTICHOKES

In Italy we have many varieties and sizes of artichokes, which are the flowers of an herbaceous plant, *Cynara scolymus*. Some are small and tender enough to be eaten raw; larger ones can be fried, boiled, or stewed. The largest, *mamme*, are stuffed and baked in the oven. Watch for fresh artichokes in produce markets in the spring and choose recipes according to which varieties are available.

BLACK CABBAGE

A winter vegetable with long green-black leaves used in such traditional Tuscan dishes as *ribollita*, black cabbage can sometimes be found in North American produce markets under the name dinosaur kale or lacinato kale.

CARDOONS

The long, pale green stalks of cardoons look something like celery but they are not related, and celery cannot be substituted. Cardoons are of the same family as thistles and artichokes. In Tuscany, they are in season throughout the cooler months. Ask for them in produce markets and good supermarkets.

CHILE PEPPER

Use the small hot red peppers smaller than your little finger, we call *peperoncini*. Chop them when they are fresh, in their season, in the spring and summer. We string them together in garlands and dry them for use the rest of the year. To us the most important parts are the seeds, which contain valuable vitamins and minerals. We grind the dried peppers, including the seeds, into a powder, and use very small quantities in all kinds of dishes. Look for powdered chile pepper in your market. Do not use paprika or cayenne pepper, which are not the same, or the product available in the United States called "chili powder," which contains other spices as well as chile.

LARDO

Lardo is pork fat prepared by pickling it for a long time in brine with herbs and spices added for flavor. It is used for cooking and is also cut into the thinnest slices and served with bread. The old-fashioned *lardo* made in the Tuscan town of Colonnata was to be banished from our tables by a misguided European Union regulation that decreed as unhygienic its traditional preservation in marble bathtubs. Fortunately, a strong public opinion movement arose to safeguard the small local productions and to prevent the extinction of this and other traditionally made Italian products. Ask for it in Italian grocery stores.

MOZZARELLA CHEESE

There are two kinds of true mozzarella, a soft, wet cheese that is kept moist in its own whey until it is used. The most famous, called *di bufala,* is made in the region of Naples with part or all buffalo milk. The other, *fiordilatte,* is made entirely from cow's milk. Mozzarella comes in various sizes, from the bite-size *bocconcino* to pieces weighing more than four pounds. It must be used very fresh, no more than two or three days from the time it is made. Buffalo mozzarella is also smoked using wheat straw. A few Neapolitan dairies in North America make mozzarella. Avoid the mass-produced stuff that is sold in plastic packages in supermarkets; it tastes more of plastic than of cheese.

NIPITELLA

Nipitella is a fresh wild herb of the mint family variously called *Satureia calamintha, Calmintha salvatica,* or *Nepeta cataria* in Latin and *nipitella* in Italian. In Tuscany, fresh *nepitella* is usually given away with the porcini, but it is not readily available everywhere and it is not replaceable. Richters Herb Specialists of Goodward, Ontario, offers seeds and plants through its Web site, www.richters.com. They will ship anywhere in the world.

OLIVE OIL

Tuscan olive oil is described at the beginning of the third chapter (see page 67). I recommend the extra virgin kind only, which is the first oil that is pressed from the olives, using the cold-pressing method. We use the oil raw as a dressing as well as for cooking. Try to buy oil only from the most recent harvest, which takes place in November and December. In Italy, the bottles and cans are stamped with the date the oil is made. This is not required everywhere, so you should ask your grocer for the date. A good grocery store will sometimes let you taste the oil. Unless you are sure the oil you are buying is fresh, you might do better to get it in clear bottles, where you can examine its color. When the oil is very fresh it is green, opaque, and fruity, with a slightly sharp

Olives

taste. As it sits in the bottle, the solids begin to settle; it gets clearer and yellower, and loses its sharpness.

ONIONS
In Tuscany, we mainly use red onions. The slightly elongated variety called Tropea is best. We occasionally use other onions, which are mentioned in the recipes that call for them.

PARMESAN CHEESE
The best Parmesan cheese comes from Reggio Emilia: It will have the words "parmigiano reggiano" stamped on the rind. It has to be aged for a minimum of two years; the date it is made should also be on the rind. Never buy it already grated, as it quickly dries out and loses its flavor. Grate it using the medium blade on a box grater; this will produce the best texture for dressing dishes; this consistency is good for melting, too.

Red onion (above)
San Marzano tomatoes
and small zucchini (right),
Porcini mushrooms (below)

PECORINO CHEESE
The sheep's-milk cheese made in Tuscany is milder than the Romano variety that is better known outside Italy, so if only the latter variety is available, you might prefer to use a little less of it than the recipes specify.

PORCINI MUSHROOMS
Porcini (*Boletus edulis*), literally "little pigs" in Italian, are wild mushrooms that grow all over Italy, and in other countries throughout the Northern Hemisphere, under oak, pine, and chestnut trees. It is relatively easy to find them dried in North America; these are the best ones for cooking, reconstituted, in sauces or with stewed meats and poultry. The fresh ones have a lighter taste and a more powerful aroma. We cook them many different ways and also eat them raw. In their season, ask for them in specialty produce markets or ask a mushroom-hunting friend.

PROSCIUTTO
Good prosciutto is sweet and intense, with a nice flavor and not too salty. Once it is sliced it must be eaten immediately, otherwise it will quickly dry out. It should be naturally aged, a process that takes at least six months. The best way to find a good one is to taste samples and decide which one you like best. Several recipes in this book call for prosciutto rinds. Ask your butcher to save you a rind, and freeze what is not used.

RICE
In Italy the preferred variety of rice is called *carnaroli*. It is medium-grained, compact, and

not likely to become mealy. Also popular is *vialone nano*, which is stumpier and slightly less compact. In any case, the best are untreated, whole-grain rices. Both of these are available in America in Italian and specialty food stores. We also use the kind called *arborio*, which may be easier to find in North America.

TOMATOES

In Italy there are many varieties of tomatoes, used for different purposes, such as sauces, salads, stuffing, and baking. Each of them is best when the locally grown tomatoes are in season and fully ripe. San Marzanos, which are slightly elongated and tapering, and *fiorentini*, which are round and deeply lobed, are the best for sauces. On page 15, I give the recipe for canning your own tomatoes. If you buy canned tomatoes in the store, choose whole, peeled San Marzano tomatoes from Italy. The labels may say "pomodori pelati San Marzano," or you can recognize them by the picture on the label. Organically grown ones are labeled *biologico*. As I have mentioned, good canned tomatoes are always an acceptable substitute for good fresh ones in cooked sauces. If a dish requires fresh tomatoes, however, only use the best, ripest, most flavorful ones, and only make the dish when tomatoes are in season.

TUSCAN-STYLE BREAD

Tuscan loaves are large and round or elongated, with a golden crust and a soft white interior. They are made without salt or fat, leavened with natural yeast, and baked in loaves of about 2 pounds (1 kg). Outside of the region, many bakeries produce Tuscan-style bread under names such as *boule*, peasant, *paesano*, Italian country, and the like, with varying degrees of success. This kind of bread should never be purchased sliced as this will cause it to dry out and lose its flavor. For more, see page 23.

VINEGAR

Whenever vinegar is mentioned in the recipes, use good-quality red wine vinegar unless another kind, such as white wine vinegar or balsamic vinegar, is specified. True balsamic vinegar, from Modena, is not really vinegar at all but a very dense liquid produced by many years of slow evaporation in wooden barrels. It is extremely expensive. Avoid the stuff sold under this name in supermarkets.

ZUCCHINI (COURGETTES)

In Tuscany we have zucchini in two shapes: round, and the better-known elongated variety. Ideally, a zucchini will be about 6 to 7 inches (15 to 18 cm) long and 1 inch (2½ cm) thick, with the blossom still attached.

acknowledgments

I want to thank the many people who have helped me along the way to make this book. Barbara and Cary Wolinsky, who gave light and life to my words. Salvatore Nasca, who translated my original Italian manuscript into English, and Ellen Hays, who translated some late additions. Amy Fonoroff and Whit Griswold, who helped to make the English clearer. Kirsty Melville and Carrie Rodrigues, of Ten Speed Press, for their expert guidance. Antonio Andreucci, whose paintings depict the atmosphere that I try to give in my writing. My crew at the Zibibbo Restaurant who supported me. But this book would have never come to life if Michael Melford had not believed in it. He has been like an obstetrician helping me through a difficult delivery.

—Benedetta Vitali

Every photographic project is a kind of happy conspiracy—like-minded people who agree to be inconvenienced by the photographer to a common end. Without these nods of cooperation, not even a sweet project on Tuscan cooking can exist. We thank the people who introduced us to the good food of Tuscany. They inspired us with their great love of life and the work they do. Our gratitude to:

Anna Vitali for introducing us to her wonderful neighbors in Antella—Maria Roschi and Anatasia Polacco for the loaning us of their kitchens; Ugo, Antonio, Primetta, Irene, and Margherita Calvelli, for graciously allowing us to intrude into their farm routines day after day.

Carla, Carlo, and Filippo Rocchi and Stefania Granger of Azienda Agricola Castelvecchio, and Toni Ballerin and Aljoscha Goldschmit of Fattoria Corzano & Paterno for showing us that the making of fine wine is indeed a way of life. Pino Demurtas for demonstrating that spectacular cheese starts with happy sheep. Giuseppe Vanni for allowing us to hug his magnificent chianinas; and Bindo Paoli for rasing his fish nets on Lake Massaciuccoli despite the rain.

Cristiana and Ottavio Calonaci for making their love of fine fruit extend across generations, Paulo Salvini for giving up a desk career to pursue his love of the land, Antonio and Loredana Lisciandro of Gelateria Carabè for making quality gelato an obsession, the maestros of I Fratellini for proving that fast food can be fine food, and Roberto Marchetti who single-handedly established a community of chestnut lovers in central Florence.

◆

The Zibibbo crew:
Armando, Cristina, Laura, Lorenzo, Mohammad, Jamie, Rozenna, Benedetta, Barbara, Kahlil, Paula, and Nicoletta.

Silvano Massi of Anzuini-Massi & C.S.N.C. and Alderigo and Emilio Triglia of Salumi Triglia for opening our senses to the rich, mellow world of cured meats; Antonio Betti of Betti and Sinatti Pasticceria for working a blizzard of magic with pastry before our eyes; and Venanzio Vannucci for granting us entrance to the ancient caves of lardo.

Julia Christe who saved us with her food styling skills; Andrea Paoli for his daily navigations through a seemingly impenetrable maze of Italian drivers; Ardelio, for sharing his secret home; John Granger and Simona Parigi for making us feel at home; and Giulio Picchi and Silvia for inspiring us with that kiss.

Michael Melford, for understanding that the essential ingredient for bringing a project to life is unbleached passion. And, most of all, to Benedetta Vitali, whose passion for wonderful food overflows every day to the great joy of the many who love her.

—Barbara and Cary Wolinsky

index